Buddha
the
Bachatero

The Eastern Wisdom
of
Latin Rhythm

BY

FRANKO

To Dr. Cochran,
Thank you for all your
support. I am forever
grateful. Frank.

Dedication

To my Father, John, who came to New York City with only $50 in 1973 and sacrificed everything for his Family to flourish.

To my Mother, Cathy, the backbone, spirit and foundation of our Family.

To my Sister, Patricia, for unconditional and unflinching love, support and understanding in all I did.

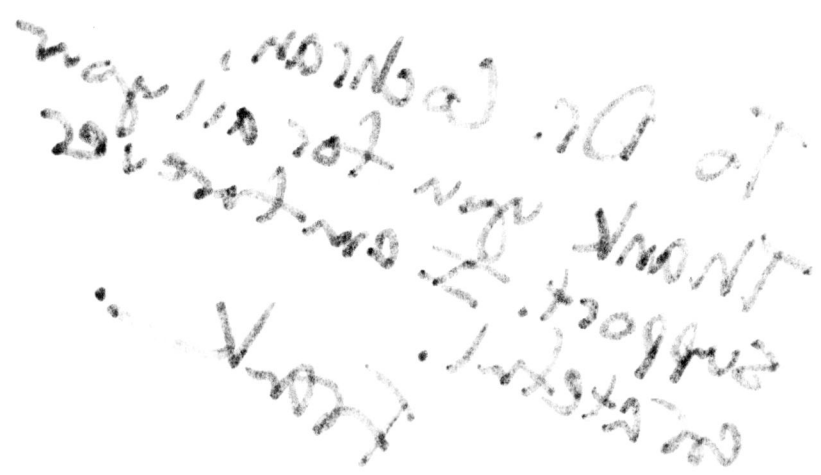

Acknowledgements

I would like to express my deepest gratitude and appreciation to the following people in chronological order for blessing my life in one way or another. Thank you all for your patience, generous guidance, energy, enthusiasm and unwavering faith during this humbling and enlightening journey of writing and completing a book. Thank you first to my entire family, Quinman Picou, Jose Alex Peralta (Big Al) and family, Robert Urena (Big Rob), Ed Urena (Ed Rock) and family, Victor Nunez, Pedro Nunez (R.I.P.), Annette Pittman, Ibzan, Lily and family, Jason Carnevale and family, Kathy Razon and family, John Ofreda and family, Sergia Louise Anderson (my first dance teacher), Enrique Sanchez and family, Danny Bahora and family, Lawrence Rodriguez and family, Betty Rodriguez and family, Edwence Georges, Jonathan Cruz and Nicole Ali and family. Also, a special thanks to Sifu Vingrove Thomas and all my training brothers at The Six Harmony Martial Arts Academy in New York City. You have all been a blessing to my life and I will forever be indebted to all of you for your unconditional love, support and understanding.

And those who were seen dancing were thought to be insane by those who could not hear the music.

- Friedrich Nietzsche

Contents

Preface

Murdered,
Are the manners,
Motives
And melodies
Of the modern man.

Always at the mercy
Of the marketplace;
Morally
And mentally molded
By money,
Media
And machines.
Masterminds
Of our own misery,
Madness
And malice.

Controlled,
And conditioned
By the contaminations
Of classrooms,
Cubicles
And the cowardly conflicts
And collisions
Of corporate combat.

Brainwashed
By the barometers of business
And business banter –
Most are just brutes,
And brawlers;
Merely mimicking
The mannerisms
And mastery of masculinity.

Selling out
To the superficial standards,
Systems
And spectacles
Of society.

Stiff like statues,
Succumbing
To social status and slavery
But still broke,
Burdened
And begging
For artificial approval,
Applause
And admiration.

Fixated
On financing phony fantasies
To further the flesh
But failing
To ever find fulfillment;
Forever flustered,
Fatigued
And frustrated.

Intoxicated
With ideals,
Icons
And images
To imitate;
Looks good so we take the bait.
Forcing us to remain inferior,
Inadequate
And incomplete.

We have become pawns
And puppets –
Predictable
And pampered.
Pushed to be productive,
Professional
And practical –
Pedaling products,
Paperwork
Protocol and profit –
But punished
By postponement
And the unforgiving wrath
Of unfulfilled,
Unattended
And unrealized romances,

Risks
And riches.

Desensitized,
And digitally dominated,
Our deeds and dialogues
Are defined by devices
And destructively delegated
To machines.
Dying daily,
From diploma
To debt,
Debt
To descending deep
Into desperation
And disappointment
Behind our desks.

This is not merely a planet
Of pain,
Pleasure
And the pursuit
Of perishable power.
We must ponder
And pursue a new path;
An unpaved path
To purity,
Peace,
Prosperity and poetry.

A new beginning,
Burning bridges
To the old burdens
And barriers
That blinded us.
Inviting internal inquiry,
Intimacy
And intensity
To breakthrough any boundaries
That have buried
The beauty and bliss
Of our bodies.

This new beginning
Is the birth of a blueprint

That I have branded
Buddha the Bachatero.

Buddha the Bachatero
Is an awakening
To artistic ascension
And abundance;
Tuning in
To the treasures
And triumphs
Of our internal terrains;
Our temple.

This blueprint
Is my elucidation
Of the expressions,
Etiquette
And energy
Of the Eastern Engine
Illuminated
By Latin limbs,
Lyrics
And love.

I am not looking
To translate the technical –
Tips, tricks, terminology
Or techniques –
But rather,
To shift
Our current emphasis
From digital dominance
And the electronic ego
To the internal intricacies
Of our individuality –
Intimacy,
Intensity,
Intent and integration.

And to examine
The equation to excellence
And enlightenment
By engaging
In the education
Of our own energies,

Emotions
And experiences.

There is no need
To pray in India,
Love in London,
Eat in Egypt
Or party in Paris.

Embody the essence
Of Buddha the Bachatero
Not as a religion, ritual or remedy,
But as a reinvention
Of the responsibilities,
Respect
And rhythms
Of the modern man.

But whether we endeavor
To groom our greatness
And grace
As a thinking,
Spiritual,
Rational
Or Renaissance man,
We must not forsaken
The fundamental foundations
Of all families,
Fortunes
And fulfillment –
That Mothers are our Masters
And we shall welcome
And worship
The warmth,
Will,
Worth and womb
Of our women.

I am going to speak some reckless words, and I want you to listen recklessly.

- Chuang Tzu, Ancient Taoist Philosopher

Shall we dance?

Introduction

Born in the Dominican Republic with the humblest of beginnings, Bachata, was a genre of music and dance that was originally unpopular, unappreciated and often deemed as vulgar and low class. Equipped with heart, hope and an indomitable spirit to be heard, Bachata persevered through the early ridicule and resistance from the more popular and prosperous styles of music such as Salsa and Merengue. *Bachateros,* or the male dancer or singer, continued to captivate small audiences through underground performances, celebrations, cassette recordings and the rare airtime that were reluctantly offered by local radio stations. Bachata would eventually evolve – breaking through to reach the popularity of mainstream media and becoming deeply embedded into the bodies, blood, breath and bones of dancers, artists and audiences all across the globe.

Bachateros became the bridge to cultivating both cultural and creative consciousness just as Buddha served to be the model for meditation and enlightenment. Siddhartha Guatama, known today as Buddha, meaning, "Awakened One," was born into his role as a prince in India. After renouncing material wealth and possessions at age 29, Buddha left his palace to seek truth. It was during this journey that Buddha famously attained enlightenment by meditating under a Bodhi tree for 49 consecutive days. Buddha shared his experiences with many disciples until his death and proclaimed to them that the root cause of all human suffering was our desiring or craving; clinging to material possessions. He expanded this teaching through the *Four Noble Truths* and revealed the remedy to dissolving our desiring through the *Eight-Fold Path* – Right Understanding, Right Thought, Right Speech, Right Action, Right Livelihood, Right Effort, Right Mindfulness and Right Concentration.

This book envisions a meeting of meditation and music – synthesizing the awakening of a Buddha and the artistry of a Bachatero. The Bachatero is the stimulus, the sensual, and the Buddha is the center. This coming together of a Buddha and a Bachatero is a blueprint blessed by the internal intricacies of Eastern energy, etiquette and excellence complemented by the emotional, lyrical and cultural command of Bachata. This is the Eastern wisdom of Latin rhythm – infusing influence from time-honored classics as the *Art of War* by supreme strategist, Master Sun Tzu, to the *Art of Peace* by the founder of Aikido, Morihei Ueshiba. From boxing to Buddha and the glorious guidance from the ancient *I-Ching* (pronounced yee-jing), also known as the *Book of Changes*. From Osho, the Indian Spiritual Mystic to the mastery of Bruce Lee, the Founder of Jeet Kune Do and one of the greatest martial artist of all time.

The *Tao Te Ching*, is the ancient Chinese text written by Lao Tzu, over 2,500 years ago. This book is one of the most translated books in the world and is highly regarded and coveted as a classic of world literature. The Tao (pronounced *Dao*), means "the Way" or "a path" – the natural course of things. Lao Tzu, roughly translated as "the old master," is considered to be the Father of Taoism. He wrote the *Tao Te Ching* with the use of penetrating poetry and profound paradox. Today, the timeless wisdom of the Tao permeates the paradigms and passages to all pursuits – the Tao of writing, running, gardening, painting, winning, skiing and sex, while continuing to cure and clarify the contemporary conflicts and conditions of our culture. One prospers with the Tao, not through prayer or praise, but in the purity of their presence and participation within the Way. As the Buddha said, "You cannot travel the path until you have become the path itself."

Each chapter of this book concludes with the mantra: Bow. Breathe. Baila Bachata. Bowing is a gesture of humility, respect, understanding and unconditional acceptance. Breathe – your breathing, your very breath, is a bond with the pulse of our planet. Your breath is the bridge to all forms of life as it harmonizes with the heart of Heaven and the energy of Earth. Baila Bachata – to dance Bachata – is to engage, explore and examine the extraordinary expressions of everyday life. Sing, celebrate and savor the strength and sincerity of our stars, sands and seas. Every moment is a dance when you awaken to artistic abundance and ascension – your very existence is a dance.

Bow. Breathe. Baila Bachata.

Buddha the Bachatero:
The Eastern Wisdom of Latin Rhythm

CONTROLLING. Control is comfort. Comfort is conformity and, ultimately, captivity to the limitations of our own creative capacity and comprehension of life, art, love and the unknown. Those seeking to control, often end up being controlled.

Because one does not want to be disturbed, to be made uncertain, he establishes a pattern of conduct, of thought, a pattern of relationships to man. He then becomes a slave to the pattern and takes the pattern to be the real thing.

- Bruce Lee, Martial Artist and Founder of Jeet Kune Do

We are only comfortable with what we can control, claim and conquer. Conditioned to be predictable and well behaved, we cling to codes, cults and karma. We pursue and pray for power over people, products and profit in hopes to secure sanity, security, significance and satisfaction. But control is merely a casual collection of commodities – cash, cars, confidence, customers, credentials – that are all impermanent, perishable and incompatible with nature, spontaneity or love. Unless one relinquishes control, relaxing will not be possible, responding to new rhythms and romances will not be possible and reinvention of the rules and routines that restricts our reality will not be possible. Everything is fixed, fabricated and familiar but often forced.

We must be willing to get rid of the life we've planned, so as to have the life that is waiting for us.

- Joseph Campbell, The Power of Myth

Control
Is a concept
That is commonly confused
With competence
Or a confirmed caliber
Of character,
Calm
And class.

A misconception of the masses
That merely
Captures the climax
Of one's comfort zone.
Conditioned

And compelled
To be clear,
Keen and critical,
We desire the discipline
To dictate
And dominate –
Canceling curiosity,
To control cash,
Climate
And colors,
Only to be caged
By conventional
Cookie-cutter conclusions.

Control is never achieved when sought after directly; it is the surprising result of letting go.

- James Arthur Ray, Writer

We are crippled by the allure of control; clinging to calculations, conveniences and choices cemented in certainty - held captive to only what we can carefully characterize. We are completely obsessed with controlling everyone and everything – friends, family, fortune, faith and fashion; mind, money and marriage. Seeking security in schedules, sex and social status. Nothing new can happen. We eat the same things everyday, repeat the same mechanical tasks and see the same people, at the same time. Control is often classified as confidence, composure and command but also commonly leads to compulsion, conflict, resistance and resentment. Everyday is just a repeat of yesterday. We are robots repeating routines, revoking our right to renew the beauty and bliss of the extraordinary expressions and energy that are embedded in the elegance of everyday. Only deep curiosities and questioning can compel the spirit and consciousness of creativity, clarity and courage – not a lustful agenda to control, accumulate and overpower.

Mastering others requires strength,
Mastering oneself is true power.

- Tao Te Ching

Katas (pronounced kah-tas), is the Japanese word meaning "form," used to describe set sequences or patterns, postures and movements that are performed and practiced in the traditional martial art of Karate. Katas are coded to carry a story, history or messages from Masters to demystify situations, spirit and wisdom to promote the perfection of character, will technique and energy.

Choreography in dance, like katas, is a crystallization of a concept, an ideology, a predetermined performance dictated by controlled confidence, conviction and conclusion. Teachers and students often spend hours on stage, in studios and schools practicing routines, "getting good" at synchronized sequences and perfecting the predictable. Staying sharp, tight and snappy while showcasing a silicone smile. This is fine for fabricating a dazzling display but only partial to the depth, dynamic dimensions and spontaneous nature of dancing.

The truth is outside of all set patterns.

- Bruce Lee, Martial Artist

From the confines of choreography and katas
To calligraphy –
Free, spontaneous, present -
Envision your bodies
As brushes,
Sweeping across the floor
As your canvas.

Each step savored
As a stroke of effortless art,
Releasing the ink - your spirit –
As you seduce,
Invite
And welcome
Your woman into a dance
That is alive,
Amplified,
Artistic and authentic.

Every stroke,
Like every step,
Is spacious,
Sensuous and sweet.
Reciprocating responses

Between your feet gracing the floor,
And the floor
Gracing your feet,
A continuous conversation,
Between feet and floor,
Floor and feet.

Walk as if you are kissing the Earth with your feet.

- Thich Nhat Hanh, Vietnamese Zen Buddhist Monk

Dancing is like surfing. Surfing is the art of surrendering. Surrendering is to simply cease all struggling and separation within ourselves so that we can unite with the Universe. Our human bodies are blessed and comprised of over 70% water, so why would we fight with what we are made out of. As any surfer would agree, any attempts to aggressively overpower the orchestra of the oceans by resisting, forcing or contesting its vigor, vitality and vastness, will undoubtedly cause collision and catastrophe. However, if a communion occurs, a seduction, oneness, then the surfer dissolves and disappears; ego is eliminated and only essence, expression and eternal energy endures.

The creative process is a process of surrender, not control.

- Julia Cameron, The Artist's Way

The wisest person
Trusts the process
Without seeking to control

- Tao Te Ching

Bachata Bond: We have reduced and cataloged our lives to learn, love, look and laugh only in proportion to what we can control. We absolutely crave control – cautious, calculating, confident - avoiding uncertainty at all costs. Control is ideology, a form of imprisonment. We must be in control because we have not leaped into a love affair with living, with the unknown, the unexpected and uncontrollable, where a deep relaxation is needed, a deep surrendering, a letting go. Trying to control everything is to be consciously denying the expressions of Existence to unfold, to unveil something special, spontaneous and distinct to your life.

We must maintain control of our income, so we stay at miserable jobs, doing the same mindless tasks day after day with people that we despise and in places that bore us, in order to secure the consistency of a paycheck, schedule and role. Same with relationships; we remain in abusive, dry and dead relationships because it allows us to control what to expect - no surprises, strenuous efforts or creativity needed. We become complacent and accustomed to these casual encounters and confrontations while concurrently deepening our desperation and despair.

Men are often instructed and encouraged to be the leader, the alpha, and control the dance, control your partner; lead the dance. Bachateros know that controlling kills the dance as well as the fragrance, feel and freedom of our women. Like surfing, any arrogant or aggressive attempts to overpower, force or control a woman to dance *your* dance, to your rhythm, timing, limitations and ego, will undoubtedly cause conflict, complexity and collision. To be in control is to be cautious and calculated. Being cautious while dancing is to not dance at all.

Only the weak and insecure, with the fabrication of force – physical, mental, sexual, emotional – can impose control and captivity to a woman just as the armor of a submarine or boat enables men to navigate the seas with complete control, charisma and confidence. But at any moment, the will of the waves can wipe out, overwhelm and overcome any armor or mechanism it so wishes. This too mirrors the will and wonder of our women. As with surfing, only a communion through surrendering is sure to seduce and satisfy the waves of a woman. One cannot control nor possess what is free. Our women are free, awakened, conscious and creative all on their own. The question is not whether we can control them, but rather can we complement, collaborate and contribute to their beauty – creatively, socially, naturally and sensually? We need to cease the cowardice confrontations with our women – condemning, condescending, controlling – and stay celebrating our women.

18

Controlling is not necessary when you carry the consciousness of a creator, awakening to all that is alive, available and abundant. The ability and awareness to create an experience, a memory, a taste, a fragrance or fire is the ultimate work of a Bachatero. Allow creativity to connect and clarify your dance, not control. If your signals are unclear, controlling is not the answer; inviting is. Invite your partner into the unknown, something that is pulsating, alive, authentic and orgasmic. Captivate and caress her curiosities, welcome her wishes as you continue to creatively contribute to the magic of the moment.

Bow. Breathe. Baila Bachata.

CORAZON (HEART). Training the head is easy. Honoring the heart is not.

All the knowledge I posses everyone else can acquire, but my heart is all my own.

- *Johann Wolfgang von Goethe, German Writer*

In a hard and hostile world,
Our heads
Are hardwired to hurry,
Hesitate
And hate.
Hardened by habits
And hurt
By the hurdles
Of our high horse.

Hoping to become heroes
And head honchos,
Making history,
Heavy hitting,
Headstrong, headfirst,
Smart,
Strategic and secure,
But we often miss the heart of the matter.

The dance of the flower in the wind, in the sun, in the rain, cannot be understood by the head; the heart has to be open for it.

- *Osho, Spiritual Mystic*

Approaching life through the head in a competitive, ambitious and ego driven world is what we have been conditioned to do; competing and comparing, cash is king, kill or be killed.

The best and most beautiful things in the world cannot be seen or even touched. They must be felt with the heart.

- *Helen Keller, American Author and Activist*

The head is easily hypnotized
But not the heart.
Engaging with the head
Is to be cold,
Cunning and calculating,

While heeding with the heart
Is to harmonize
With the ways of heaven.

The best work is done with the heart breaking, or overflowing.

- Mignon McLaughlin, American Author

The heart breaks
But houses humor
And humility
To heal holistically;
To expand.
While the head aches
And hallucinates,
Hardening in hardships
While our happiness
And health
Are held hostage.

The heart has its reasons which reason knows not.

- Blaise Pascal, French Writer

The heart jumps,
The head judges,
Your head is in your hands,
Your heart,
In the hands of heaven.

The *Upanishads,* a collection of sacred texts and teachings of
Hinduism and Buddhism states, "Communication is head-to-
head; a communion is heart-to-heart."

The heights of your heart,
Each beat beckons beauty,
Bonding
With the body,
Breath,
And beauty
Of our brides,
Beaus
And bachateras.

When one is so absolutely relaxed that there is no tension either in the body or in the mind, then suddenly there is an opening of the heart. Only in total relaxation does the heart open, it becomes a flower.

- Osho,

Bachata Bond: Bachata is the art of dancing with the heart, not the head. Happiness, health and harmony are all in the beat of your heart not in the bondages and barriers of your head. Hurry and hesitation never hinders the heart. Only the head is burdened with technique, timing, imitation and insecurities.

Our women can easily tell the difference between one who dances with their head as opposed to their heart. Much like a kiss, dance reveals much. We have an opportunity to offer our hearts, to let it melt into the moment, in hopes to meet the hearts of our women.

Bow. Breathe. Baila Bachata.

EYE CONTACT. The elegance, enjoyment and empowerment of our eyes have evolved into mere extensions of our ego.

What you see depends on how you see the world...to most people, dirt is just dirt, but to the farmer of life, it's potential.

- Doe Zantamata, Writer

Enslaved by ego,
Our eyes are exhausted.
Entertained
But blank,
Not engaged.
Enchanted
By excess and expediency,
The envious eye endeavors only to escape,
Evading existence,
Examination
And the equation
To enlightenment.

A man sees in the world what he carries in his heart.

- Johann Wolfgang von Goethe, German Writer

No fire in our eyes,
Our senses are buried,
Technologically heavy,
Our lives,
Love and hope,
Everything hurried.

No longer electric
Or an element of eternal energy,
Our eyes are extinguished,
Fearful
And fixated on falsities,
Crusty
And closed like a corpse.

The five colors blind the eye.
Therefore the Sage
Takes care of the belly,
Not the eye.

- Tao Te Ching

The *Tao Te Ching* references the five colors – green, red, yellow, white, black – and observes how easily we are blinded and brainwashed by the spectacles of society and superficial stimulus. Easily enchanted by ego-driven entertainment and expensive things, we only see the surface and cannot penetrate past the perimeter and into the poetry of people, places and the present. Therefore, the Ancient Chinese Sages consulted their "belly" (or their center) for truth, guidance, honesty and feeling.

My heart burns like fire but my eyes are as cold as dead ashes."

- Soyen Shaku, Zen Master

Eye contact is brief,
Brisk,
Biased and blurry.
We look
But only in lust,
Lies and limitations.
Eyes
wandering in weakness;
Not wonder,
Enslaved
From endless escaping.

Let others see their own greatness when looking in your eyes.

- Mollie Marti, American Writer and Teacher

No longer do our eyes offer an effortless exchange of eternal energy but rather only as an output of egotistic efforts to entice eyeballs, to command attention and showcase our significance.

Art is not what you see, but what you make others see.

- Edgar Degas, French Artist

The Zen concept of "New Eyes" encourages us to examine, envision and engage in every moment, activity or relationship with an uncontaminated, unblemished and undisturbed view, one that is not stuck in the past or anxious of the future; without discrimination or preconceived notions. The Five Eyes of Buddhism – the corporeal eye (physical), the clairvoyant eye (intuitive), the eye of wisdom, the eye of objective truth, the eye of enlightenment – also fosters the full spectrum of sight and perception to promote clarity.

The most pathetic person in the world is some one who has sight but no vision.

- Helen Keller, American Author

Bachata Bond: Bachata is the art of seeing and savoring the unseen, the Invisible. Seeing past the predictable, the pretentious and physical and into the Infinite. How we look at something and what we choose to see are both deeply rooted in our conditioning – social, cultural, psychological. Even with the abilities to penetrate precisely, panoramically, peripherally while concurrently utilized as both microscope and telescope, our eyes are easily deceived, distracted, discriminatory and now destructively dumbed down due to a digital dominance of devices and screens.

We cannot express and evolve into what we envision because we lack insight, we are dark, desperate and dormant within. We are limited and imprisoned exclusively by external enticement. We must elevate above eye-level. See past the naked eye, enhanced eye and even the "third eye." Literally, look up to the skies and experience the elimination of ego, the bondages of your boredom, burdens and brainwashing. Cleanse.

In Bachata, we are deceived and distracted by the disguise of sexual stimulus, status and style. We must dance blindfolded, either literally or metaphorically, and dance with the intelligence, intuition and instincts of our belly. Seeing and seducing with our stomach. We often close our eyes as we encounter extreme emotional experiences – relief, joy, jubilation, sadness and success, victory and defeat – to gather a glimpse of truth and feeling. We must engage our eyes as receptors of eternal energy, enthusiasm and emotion and embrace the elegance of our women with New Eyes, not the envious or egotistical eye.

Bow. Breathe. Baila Bachata.

INDIVIDUALITY. Insecurity and imitation are the root causes of internal illiteracy. They insistently intervene with the art of illuminating individuality.

The Tao teaches,
To know The Way,
Understand the great within yourself.

- Lao Tzu

This is a society infested
With illusions of influence,
Affluence
And decadence;
Immersed
In the impurities
Of institutional ideology,
Through idols,
Icons
And images.

To be yourself in a world that is constantly trying to make you something else is the greatest accomplishment.

- Ralph Waldo Emerson, American Author and Poet

By chasing trends,
Gimmicks
And lifestyles,
We become more impersonal,
Imitative
And impotent as ever.
Captured
In the crossroads
Of internal confusion,
Conflict
And chaos.

Our lives are not as limited as we think they are; the world is a wonderfully weird place; consensual reality is significantly flawed; no institution can be trusted, but love does work; all things are possible; and we all could be happy and fulfilled if we only had the guts to be truly free and the wisdom to shrink our egos and quit taking ourselves so damn seriously.

- Tom Robbins, American Author

Chasing public perception,
Internal deception,
Self-decapitate,
Every time you imitate,
The poison you perpetuate,
The fiction you formulate,
Brainwashed,
Taking the bait.

In order to be irreplaceable, one must always be different.

- Coco Chanel, French Fashion Designer

The imbalances
Of an imitative identity -
Insecure, impatient, immature –
Inducing
A narcissistic necessity
To impose
And impress,
Gaining social proof
And prominence,
Accumulating artificial attention,
Approval
And applause.

Keep seeking approval,
And you will be chained.

- Tao Te Ching

Living distorted lives through the illusions
Of roles,
Ranks and reputation –
Robotic
And replaceable.
Influenced
By the ideology
Of institutions –
Religious, educational, political, corporate –
Mesmerizing
The mechanical minds
Of mediocre men;
Mass marketing
The maps of money,

27

Masculinity,
Worship
And wellness.

Reputation is what men and women think of us; character is what God and angels know of us.

- *Thomas Paine, English-American Philosopher*

We are trying too hard to posses an image, to own some kind of identity, to impose our influence and imitative ideas on people, products and places. We are impersonating impressions of greatness through gimmicks, accepting ourselves even for things that we are not; doing things that we do not want to do, with people that we do not want to do it with and in places that we do not want to be and behaving through beliefs that we do not believe in.

Whatever games are played with us, we must play no games with ourselves.

- *Ralph Waldo Emerson, American Poet*

Domesticated
Deceived
And demoralized
By the systems
And shackles of society,
We ponder,
Pursue
And impersonate personalities
To survive.

The most courageous act is still to think for yourself. Aloud.

- *Coco Chanel*

Imprisoning
And intensifying
An incremental infringement
On our internal instruments –
Intelligence,
Intuition
And instincts.

I will not let anyone walk through my mind with their dirty feet.

- Mahatma Gandhi, Indian Activist and Leader

The branding of lifestyles, status and significance, through millions of mass marketing initiatives – television, books, magazines, medicine – have dictated our realities, fantasies, darkest desires of decadence and dominance in addition to our deepest deprivations. We are drowned with doctrines of socially acceptable ways to behave, accessories to accumulate, who to worship and the superficial standards of how men and women should look and feel. The intention is to impose images and ideals for the masses to idolize, to chase and to formulate a perception that one is always inadequate, incomplete and imperfect and must improve based on theses standards and schemes. The scattered, torn and divided Man is weak; the individual – illuminated, intimate, intense, winning from within – is a warrior and cannot be wobbled.

This above all: to thine own self be true.

- William Shakespeare, Hamlet

Individuality is the Art of Invincibility.

Invincibility
Is the art of becoming inaccessible,
Inexplicable
And impenetrable.

I'm not in this world to live up to your expectations and you're not in this world to live up to mine.

- Bruce Lee

Impervious
To the mind manipulation
Of the masses,
Incapable
Of being induced
To ignore one's inner design,
Remaining intact
To the treasures,
Technologies
And truth
Of one's internal temple.

Invincibility is a matter of defense.

- Master Sun Tzu, The Art of War

The wisdom of knowing while being unknown is vital to the Art of Invincibility and to success and victory in warfare. Master Sun Tzu states that those who are skilled in attack, their opponents do not know where to defend. In the case of those skilled in defense, their opponents do not know where to attack. Casual and contaminating campaigns to compel crowds into fear, envy and greed cannot penetrate the creativity and courage of an integrated and illuminated individual.

Be extremely subtle, even to the point of formlessness. Be extremely mysterious, even to the point of soundlessness. Thereby you can be the director of the opponent's fate.

- Master Sun Tzu

Reaching Formlessness, while inducing opposing armies to take form, while you yourself are formless, is the strategy of a victorious army. Strengths and weaknesses are a matter of formation. As Master Sun Tzu teaches, "Only the Formless cannot be affected."

If there is no enemy within, the enemy outside can do us no harm.

- African Proverb

Corporate institutions are notorious for deploying arrogant agendas and antics to exploit, control and manipulate the formations that we so freely expose. We reveal formations that forecast our desperation, dependence and fixations to fear, money, ego, greed and jealousy. Most people are easily controlled and taken advantage of because they are living paycheck-to-paycheck and are obviously willing to do anything, including taking abuse and being overworked, to make more money. An ambitious employee looking to rise in rank and recognition can easily be abused to feel inadequate, unfit and undeserving of achievement, thereby slowing progress and promotion. By institutions imposing threats and intimidation, one remains imprisoned through insecurities and guilt. "Though effective, appear ineffective." Master Sun Tzu's strategy of being Formless immobilizes any device or intent to attack one's individuality; subduing all schemes, scandals and sabotage. All that you reveal can and will undoubtedly be used to exploit and exhaust the energy, efforts and expressions that you exude.

The inner condition of the formless is inscrutable, whereas that of those who have adopted a specific form is obvious. The inscrutable win, the obvious lose.

- General Du Mu, Chinese Military General

Individuality
Is innovating from our internal intricacies –
Instincts,
Intuition
And intelligence.
Then one becomes irreplaceable,
Incomparable
And inaccessible.
No longer a slave,
Servant,
Soldier or a sacrificial sucker
To social science,
Nor to the superficial systems
And standards
Of society.

Know yourself, know your opponents;
One hundred battles, one hundred victories.

- Master Sun Tzu

The individual
Is internally instructed
And integrated,
Remaining immune
To invasive
And indecent infatuations;
Inviting intense
And instantaneous illumination,
Ensuring an immortal imprint.

The key to immortality is first living a life worth remembering.

- Bruce Lee

Bachata Bond: Individuality can be summed up by the following excerpt from an interview with Bruce Lee, in 1971 on the Pierre Burton show. Feel free to replace the word "Martial Arts" with Bachata:

To me, ultimately, Martial Arts means honestly expressing yourself. Now it is very difficult to do. I mean it is easy for me to put on a show and be cocky and be flooded with a cocky feeling and feel pretty cool and all that or I can make all kinds of phony things, blinded by it or do some fancy movement, but to express oneself honestly, not lying to oneself, that my friend, is very hard to do.

- Bruce Lee, 1971 Interview with Pierre Burton

Bow. Breathe. Baila Bachata.

WORKING HARD. We are trying too hard. Enslaved and exhausted everyday; embattled, embarrassed and enraged every evening.

It is not what the artist does that counts, but what he is.

- Pablo Picasso

The fatigue of your fight,
Never taking flight.
Misusing muscle and might,
Remaining raw,
Never ripe.

We are trying too hard.
Superficial searching,
Struggling
And sacrificing
For the silly spectacles
Of social significance
And superficial self-satisfaction.

Lusting
To legitimize our labor.
Posing and posturing
For relevance and reassurance
By chasing cash,
Climbing ladders
And conforming
To corporate conditioning.

Corporate corpse,
Unconscious,
And caught in the crossfire
Of cowardice commercial combat;
Contributing to the carnage,
Collisions
And collapses
Of contaminated capitalism.

Too many people spend money they earned to buy things they don't want to impress people that they don't like.

- Will Rogers, Performer

The cash you covet,
Pawns and puppets,
Submitting to authority,
Soul and Spirit secondary,
Conformity is your king,
Boredom your boss.
True wealth,
You will never come across.

Dominated by the demands
And desires of others,
Dying to change their minds
About who you are,
What you represent
And what you can be;
Proving your worth,
Competence
And value.

A turbulent tryst chasing titles,
Temporary treasures
And trends,
Leaving a treacherous
Trail of tears,
Tragedy
And torment towards the throne.

It is usually not until after tragedy, tears, loss or learning of a
lump that one awakens to appreciate their legs, laughter and
loved ones.

Brainwashed to stay busy,
Breadwinning through boredom
And staying buried in business bloodshed,
Betrayal
And blame
But still broke and bankrupt;
Only bankrolling more burdens
To brain and body.

It is not enough to be busy. So are the ants. The question is: What
are we busy about?

- Henry David Thoreau, American Author and Poet

The marketplace has dictated,
Deceived
And degraded
The magnificence of Man
By monetizing mechanical,
Menial
And mindless
Missions,
Motives and daily duties
That are desensitizing
Spirit and soul.

Anybody can get a job. It takes a real man to make it without working.

- Charles Bukowski, German Poet

We are driven
By mainstream media,
Money
And material.
Mass manipulated
By man-made methods
Of measuring the meaning,
Morals
And merit of Man.
All serving as mechanisms
To emphasize misery,
Mediocrity
And malice;
Further enabling exploitation,
Exhaustion
And enslavement.

You are part of the rat race because you are letting them treat you like a rat. This is the modern definition of a slave.

- Saurabh Sharma, Indian Poet

Wearing masks, suits, and costumes to work, dying at our desks, demoralized by our daily duties and dialogues that depletes and destroys our dimples. We are unhappy because this is unnatural, uncomfortable and unhealthy. We remain unconscious – asleep, stiff and servants to the artificial architecture and hierarchies of society.

The era of the elitist executive
And the entitlement to enslave,
Exploit
And exhaust the efforts,
Energy,
Earnings and enthusiasm
Of Man has ended.

Their deceit, destruction and disguise have been decoded and
decapitated.

THE EVOLUTION OF THE EASTERN ENGINE HAS
EMERGED.

The embodiment of the Eastern Engine
Is an all-encompassing expression
Of eternal energy
And enlightenment;
Beyond the barriers
Of the body
And the restrictions
Of any religion
Race
Or ritual.

Embody the emotions,
Etiquette,
And essence
Of enlightenment and excellence
Engage the elegance
Of everyday expressions
With eternal
And effortless energy.

Eliminate
Every effort enchanted by envy,
Excess
And expediency
And graduate
From the gridlock of the grind;
The grip of government.

Societies need self-sacrificing ignorant crowds;
Religions need fearful followers;
Systems need obedient slaves;

Corporate world needs compulsive consumers, and
I need the courage to rise above these four parasites.

- Saurabh Sharma, Indian Poet

No pain no gain,
Efforts die in vain,
Driven insane,
Results no different,
Life remains the same.

"No pain, no gain" does not mean that pain systematically equals
gain. It's easy to go hard. It's hard to go smart.

- Erwan LeCorre, Lifestyle Activist

Greatness,
Is not about your grind
On the grid.
Give up the garbage –
Gadgets, gimmicks, gossip –
And lay genuine groundwork
To greatness.

Greatness is doing the hardest thing with the greatest of ease.

- Cus D'Amato, Boxing Trainer
of Former Heavyweight Champion, Mike Tyson

Gambling
Through the gradations of greatness,
Grieving over glamour,
Greed
Glory and gain.

We must give up greed,
Guilt,
And grief
To be guided by generosity,
Grace
And gratitude.

The Holy Grail of Greatness
Is gratitude for the Gift –
The Gift of Godliness.

Godliness
Is our consciousness
And courage to create –
Awakening
To our abilities to ascend
Into artistic abundance
To procreate,
Produce poetry
And manifest monuments,
Music
And meaning.

We can't get It
Because we already got It,
Get inside and grasp It,
Then give It.

God is not somebody else.

- Thomas Merton, Spiritual Teacher

We are all gifted with Godliness.
We often get a glimpse
But most choose not to open the Gift,
Leaving untapped,
Unfulfilled
And unattended greatness
To our graves.

There is no greater agony than bearing an untold story inside
you.

- Maya Angelou, African-American Author and Poet

Laboring lethargically,
Working hard
To cultivate socially acceptable levels
Of confidence,
Concentration,
Cash and charisma;
Ultimately giving up,
Giving in
And gassing out.

W.O.R.K. = With Out Regret Knocking

Win from within,
Walk away from wages
And welcome
Unlimited wealth
And wellness
By waking up
To your wings,
Will
And wisdom within.

Bachata Bond: Working, for most, is a battle, a burden and is usually associated with boredom. Working to survive, to make a living, to secure a future - painful, torturing, condescending and controlling - long hours of laboring but lackluster and lacking life, creativity, change and challenge. Society associates blood, sweat and tears with significance and success so we are conditioned and compelled to chase, to accumulate and to gain; to always be occupied. We kill ourselves to cultivate the charisma, confidence and cash to satisfy the superficial standards of society. We unconsciously comply and contribute to this conditioning with careless consent, without suspicion or examination, and continue to compete and compare our competence in any craft, any category – combat, comedy, cycling or cinema. Drop this deceptive doctrine; this slogan for success and you will dissolve your dependency, depression and desperation to "work hard."

Bachata, as in life, is not about working hard – struggling, suffering, sacrificing; long labor. We do not dance hard. We do not paint hard, cook hard. Those who try hard and work hard are rigid, robotic, tense and awkward. They constantly feel the need to force, manipulate and overpower. Bachateros dance; fluid, free and unrestricted. Intimacy and intensity are intrinsic and effortless as we relax into the music and respond spontaneously to every movement and moment with our women. Bachata is an artistic, cosmic and emotional awakening. Dancing Bachata is congruent to dancing with any craft, either you are responding, flowering, loving, living and laughing or not. There is no need for forced or fabricated efforts to "work hard, " "go hard," or "try hard."

There is no duality between working and playing – working is playing and playing is working. Dancing is loving and loving is dancing.

Bow. Breathe. Baila Bachata.

CREATING. At the climax of all chaos, conflict and change, there is an opening for creating and creativity.

To be creative means to be in love with life. You can be creative only if you love life enough that you want to enhance its beauty, you want to bring a little more music to it, a little more poetry to it, a little more dance to it.

- *Osho*

The *I-Ching* or *The Book of Changes* introduced the Creative and the Receptive as the two forces that permeated and manifested all the existent and non-existent patterns of the Universe. The Creative, or Yang energy, correlates with the Heavens, also referred to as the Masculine (the Sun), characterized by strength, firmness and penetrating while the Receptive, or Yin energy corresponds with the Earth or the Female (the Moon) – flexible, nurturing and receiving. When aroused and activated by the Creative, the Receptive brings birth and beauty of all things. So Ancient Taoist Masters taught that when Yin culminates, Yang is born and when there is Yang within Yin, " a companion comes." The companion is creativity or "the living potential" which cannot surface without the illuminated interaction and oneness of Yin and Yang. Creativity and Receptivity are reflections of the continuous circulation of internal and external energies in accord with Above and Below. It is the joining and expression of this unified energy that captures the quality of creativity.

The fight is won or lost far away from witnesses – behind the lines, in the gym and out there on the road, long before I dance under the lights.

- Muhammad Ali, The G.O.A.T. and Former Heavyweight Boxing Champion of the World

Our very existence has become a daily stampede of wishes, hopes and dreams taking over our hearts, minds and prayers. Always asking, hoping and wishing but rarely receiving. We yearn but never yield, never allowing the Creative and Receptive to take its course, to collaborate. Our quality of Receptivity is often obstructed by the roadblocks of "reality," reasoning, rationality and logic. We are constantly resisting and repelling all types of blessings, energies and messages that were solely meant to uplift and advance our will, worth and wellness. But receiving is not an outward performance –

begging, imposing, forcing – while going around living with a closed fist. As in dance, one must first start with an open palm in order to invite, welcome and receive their partner.

The most important part begins even before you put your hand on the sword.

- D.Z. Hideaki, Master Swordsman

To know yang and to be true to yin
Is to echo the universe.

- Tao Te Ching

Receptivity, our ability, awareness and right to receive, reflects the miracle of growing a tree. First, the seeds (our intent, awareness, sincerity) are planted in the soil; soft, yielding and ready to receive nourishment from both the sincerity of the sun and the strength of storms. The Ancient Chinese loved to use roots and trees as an analogy to life because they knew that once the roots start to grow and penetrate deep and wide into the soil, the tree can grow as high as it wants. As Nietzsche said, "If a tree wants to reach the sky, its roots need to go to the very hell." Once the roots begin to penetrate and the tree is growing, creativity starts to sprout; spontaneous and subtle, flowers start to open and overflow naturally and abundantly.

Sadness gives depth. Happiness gives height. Sadness gives roots. Happiness gives branches. Happiness is like a tree going into the sky, and sadness is like the roots going down into the womb of the earth. Both are needed, and the higher a tree goes, the deeper it goes, simultaneously. The bigger the tree, the bigger will be its roots. In fact, it is always in proportion. That's its balance.

- Osho

Contaminated
By a culture of "clicking"
And compulsive consuming,
We have carelessly cultivated
A nation of conformists,
Copycats
And corporate corpses.

Controlled by cash,
Credit,
Cubicles and commerce,
We are conditioned to compare
And compete,
Crumbling to confusion,
Contradiction
Conflict
And scarcity;
While creativity
Remains
In captivity.

> When you realize there is nothing lacking,
> The whole world belongs to you.
>
> - Tao Te Ching

Scarcity is a man-made dynamic. It is a gimmick, a game to tame, take and exploit the efforts, earnings and enthusiasm of Man. Scarcity does not exist in nature, there is only abundance.

Operating from finite resources
And commodities – time, money, material, long labor -
While carrying a container
Of contrived confidence,
Charisma
And calm;
Recycling a ruthless
And relentless race
To stay relevant.

Creation is a better means of self-expression than possession; it is through creating, not possessing, that life is revealed.

> *- Vida D. Scudder, American Writer*

One who is not able to create ultimately conforms. One who conforms becomes only a critic at best – criticizing, complaining and condemning but never creating. As Osho reminds us, "Unless there is more than enough, man will always be exploited by man. So create more than enough, be creative, use all possibilities to create more." And "more" is not about quantity but quality; it reflects a state of

appreciation and awareness to natural abundance. Drop the
outward performances and personalities, as they only further
perpetuate poverty – internal, external and economical.

Arrive and awaken
To abundance.
Let go of lack
And lock into the love of life
Through creating and creativity.
Design
And redesign
Your destiny
And ditch your dependence
On dollars.

Remove all meaningless methods
And motivations
To manipulate,
Force
Or overpower
And start creating –
Contributing,
Collaborating
And co-existing.

Creativity is the greatest rebellion in existence.

- Osho

Jiro Ono is a world-renowned sushi chef who is the creator of
a 10 seat, sushi-only restaurant called Sukiyabashi Jiro,
located in a Tokyo, Japan, inside a subway station. Despite its
discreet and unusual location, humble square footage and
non-existent marketing, it is the first restaurant of its kind to be
recognized and awarded the coveted three-star Michelin
Guide rating. Sushi lovers, travelers, explorers, critics and
celebrities from around the globe book months in advance
and dish out top dollar to experience a meal with Chef Jiro. As
an artist, father, student and master of the culinary arts and
sushi, Chef Jiro has transcended and elevated past the
elementary conflicts and collisions of contemporary
commercial competition, commerce and combat. His craft is
cemented in spontaneity, simplicity and sincerity; a daily
celebration of soul, spirit and sushi. He is not merely earning
a living, working for wages or faking a career, he is creating a

living; the curator of his own creative climax. Unburdened by greed and contaminations of capitalism, Chef Jiro is not concerned about leases, lenders or location. People will find him, wherever he goes and they will wait, wish and wonder as he caresses his canvas; there is no menu, you eat according to his creativity in the moment. Every experience is a surprise, new and spontaneous.

Life isn't about finding yourself. Life is about creating yourself.

- George Bernard Shaw, Irish Playwright

Competition ceases,
When creativity unfolds
And unveils to us
A cosmic,
Cultural
And courageous comprehension
Of our own creative consciousness.

An idea that is not dangerous is unworthy of being called an idea at all.

- Oscar Wilde, Irish Writer and Poet

The capacity and consciousness to create is the quality of love and Godliness. This is the highest level of spirituality. To create on Earth is to be in harmony with Heaven. Enter the elevated echelons of creation and existence by engaging in the extremes of our energies, emotions and the eloquence of everyday expressions – the aroma, acoustics and artistry of nature. Create where you are, as truth is already within you. Gestures and geography will not help if you have not yet awakened to the artistic abundance that is accessible and available to you in the present moment.

A creative person is one who has insight, who can see things nobody else has ever seen before, who hears things that nobody has ever heard before – then there is creativity.

- Osho

Bachata Bond: It is easy to pursue a pre-paved, pre-determined path – working, painting, acting and dancing according to the expectations and conclusions of others. But to pave your own path, dancing to the tune of your own truth, is to embrace the choices, challenges and changes of a champion; a creator. When you are creating, everything slows down; you realize that there is no need to hurry, that no one can beat you because you are pure consciousness, pure energy; unburdened by the tools, tricks and timing of society. Clocks, calendars and computers cannot confine or control you, as you are no longer a casualty of conditioning. Like with Chef Jiro, there is no competition. He is not a part of that machine, that man-made mess we call the marketplace. He has elevated above the commercial conflicts of crowds and cowards. You cannot compete with individuals that go all-in to reinvent the rhythms to their own realities; to pave their own paths. With your own creativity, you can also capture a level of consciousness, which will eliminate and elevate above all competition as well.

As a Bachatero, you are a Creator. Creating experiences, music, memories and moments with our women and with people all over the world. Many dancers overcompensate for their inability to create and settle for comparing, controlling, dictating and dominating the dance; leading as the aggressor, the alpha. Allow creativity to take its course, as it always promises to pave a path and participate in the power of your presence. Experience something new; let the unknown unfold. As Bruce Lee said, "Ultimately, for me, martial arts is honestly and completely expressing myself, not lying to oneself." This is the highest work of a Bachatero.

Creativity is courage.

　- Henri Matisse, Artist

Bow. Breathe. Baila Bachata.

COURAGE. Courage is a celebration. It is a special switch, a spirit that seduces the unknown. Courage is the capacity to connect, create and respond – internally, spiritually, artistically, truthfully – to an internal inquiry, a challenge, a lover or a moment.

Courage is a love affair with the unknown.

> *- Pablo Picasso*

Here is where the unknown is unveiled,
Fully disclosed.
Courage is to remain open,
Never closed.

The people who are trying to make this world worse are not taking the day off. Why should I?

> *- Bob Marley, Reggae Artist*

Courage
Is not merely a campaign
To convince
And coerce yourself
Into a state of fearlessness
Or bravery.

Courage isn't having the strength to go on – it is going on when you don't have strength.

> *- Napoleon Bonaparte, French Military Leader*

Cowards looking to capture the crown,
Commercial courage,
Deficient deep down.

Constantly pounding their chest,
Artificial and aggressive,
Confrontational at best.
Not a factor,
Feeble,
Crumbling like the rest.

Life shrinks or expands in proportion to one's courage.

> *- Anais Nin, Novelist*

The countless complications
That chronicles the lives of cowards;
Forceful with friends
And family
But cordial with co-workers,
Customers
And other cowards.

Crippled
By cravings
To claim credit
And compensation,
Gravitating towards greed,
Gossip,
Games and gimmicks.

Let go over a sheer cliff. Die completely and then come back to life – after that no one can deceive you.

- Zen Proverb

Bushido, the Japanese spirit and code for martial artists and samurai's, cultivated courage through a commitment to death. Ancient warriors were taught and trained to keep the notion and possibility of death at the forefront of their daily lives and duties. This sensitivity, awareness and acceptance of death ensured that everyday embodied the full extent of one's expressions, capabilities and loyalty; giving significance to every word, thought, meal, action and interaction. Therefore, choosing death over life was never a matter of confusion or deep thought, but rather a path to truth, totality, honor, heart and fulfillment of *dharma* (a term in Buddhism referring to one's original nature and obligations in the forms of duty, service or tradition).

I'm a man who believes that I died 20 years ago. And I live like a man who is dead already. I have no fear whatsoever of anybody or anything.

- Malcolm X, Civil Rights Leader

Cowards operate in the form of crowds, unconscious and inconsiderate, cutting throats, casting stones and constantly condemning and criticizing. Courage is a creative advancement in consciousness and an absolute commitment to the unknown; whatsoever comes our way. Courage is only possible through the deepest levels of relaxation, awareness and intimacy. Use death as an analogy, as an understanding to be whole, complete and fully engaged everyday, not compromising and succumbing to cowardice tendencies – quitting, blaming, gossiping, scheming, hating. If you knew that you had one week to live, you would immediately shift your energy and enthusiasm towards all that is alive, authentic and abundant. You would immediately attend to all the things that you were previously too afraid or closed-minded to attempt. You would waste not another moment holding onto anything silly, superficial or selfish. All your worthless worries would suddenly dissipate. Your happiness would no longer be hurried, hypothetical or held hostage by the hurdles of your habits. You would be in a total state of surrender, completely open to all opportunities and possibilities of travel, action, creativity and love. It is when we hold on tight to time, our daily temptations and temporary treasures - terrified, tense, timid, - that we become trapped in the burdens of loss, greed, fear and envy. Buddha was said to be a murderer and a mother because he had to first "kill" all of your clinging, conditionings and cravings before nourishing your rebirth into consciousness and awareness.

Throughout the centuries there were men who took the first steps down new roads armed with nothing but their own vision. Their goals differed, but they all had this in common: that the step was first, the road new, the vision unborrowed, and the response they received – hatred. The great creators – the thinkers, the artists, the scientists, the inventors – stood alone against the men of their time. Every great new thought was opposed. Every great new invention was denounced. The first motor was considered foolish. The airplane was considered impossible. The power loom was considered vicious. Anesthesia was considered sinful. But the men of unborrowed vision went ahead. They fought, they suffered and they paid. But they won.

- Ayn Rand, The Fountainhead

Hate is usually hidden.
An internal burden,
Harming our homes,
Hearts,
Hands and humor.

We begin to depend
On the very hate
That plagues our potential.
We hate our jobs
But depend on its paycheck,
We hate our relationships
But depend on the comforts
And conveniences
Of our daily confrontations.

He who cannot dance claims the floor is uneven.

- Hindu Proverb

Cleanse and clarify,
Cure yourself
Of the contaminations
Of commercial courage;
Never a need to step on others
To claim
And conquer.
Remove all reasons
To mingle with copycats,
Cowards
And corporate carbon copies.

Heal your head
Of all hate,
By harmonizing your heart
With the heavens.

This is what I believe...and I'm willing to die for it. Period. It's that simple.

- Will Smith, Actor

Bachata Bond: The early days of Bachata endured extreme economical, social and political opposition. Bachateros did not resort to the blind bravery of brutes, barbarians and brawlers; bullying and blaming for advancement and approval. The courage of a Bachatero was not dependent on conflict or confrontation, but rather on an unwavering and unflinching commitment to their culture, music and message through continuous creativity in the face and furnace of the unknown; capturing tears, truth and triumph in every tune. This is the courage of a Bachatero.

Bow. Breathe. Baila Bachata.

COUNTING. Numbers are everywhere. They have influenced and nourished every element of the Universe - science, medicine, religion, art – and have revealed information for Existence to evolve, prosper and change. But the obsession for numbers – calculations, systems, metrics and percentages – has become the ultimate agent for control, manipulation, deception and violence.

Not everything that counts can be counted, and not everything that can be counted counts.

- Albert Einstein

Corporations and capitalists
Fixated on forcing,
Forecasting
And fabricating financial futures;
Consumers
In captivity of cash,
Commerce
And credit.

Conditioned,
Controlled
And carried
Into the corridors
And crossroads of class,
Conflict,
Crime
And corruption.

Numbers
Are worshipped in many forms -
Money, time, dates, rituals -
Numbers associated with art,
Architecture
And astrology.
Utilized in business,
To exploit and exhaust
The efforts,
And essence
Of Man.

Man-made systems – interest rates,
Stock markets and loans –

Manipulating minds,
Muscles,
Motives and morals,
Securing servants
And slaves to calculations –
Dependent,
Dormant
And easily dominated.

Learn the rules like a pro, so you can break them like an artist.

- Pablo Picasso

Pythagoras said, "All things are numbers." Like many ancient cultures, systems or schools, Eastern mystics also utilized numbers to mirror the rhythms of the Universe and used it as a map and a tool to navigate deeper into the origins of existence, art and humanity. *Maya*, in Buddhism, is a term that means an illusion, often the illusion of measurement; describing how men were mesmerized by the measurement and management of time, age, distance and technology. However, the narrative of numbers must return to its original nature – insightful, dynamic, honest – to fulfill its true purpose in assisting the evolution of energy and environment, the erection of monuments and demystifying and mirroring the mysteries and miracles of mankind.

The best calculation is the absence of calculation.

- Pablo Picasso

Creativity and courage
Are captured
Not in the capacity to calculate,
But in the quality
Of consciousness.

An awareness
To awaken the aftermath,
To access the innumerable,
Immeasurable
And the Infinite;
That which cannot be measured,

Captured
Or controlled
Through calculation
Or accumulation.

Muhammad Ali, former heavyweight boxing champion and considered to be one of the greatest of all time, was once asked by a reporter, "How many sit-ups can you do?" Ali responded, "I don't know, I only start counting after I can't do anymore." Quantity is irrelevant towards the transcendence of one's deepest dimensions and expressions of love and art.

Don't count the days, make the days count.

   - Muhammad Ali, Boxing Legend

Bachata Bond: Counting is often utilized and encouraged as one learns or practices Bachata. There is a basic eight count that governs this dance and provides the framework for classes, routines and choreography. However, one must transcend past all numbers and counting to free the dance, to allow it to unfold. Bachata is alive – dynamic, pulsating, vibrating - and cannot be held captive to counting as it makes you awkward, tense, robotic, rigid and cold.

Moments of triumph and truth always showers upon us beyond any man-made methods of measurements, calculations and formulas.

Bachateros have taken and continue to take measures that are immeasurable. We take all measures to manifest miracles and magic for our women - to merge and melt into their wishes and warmth. This cannot be captured through calculation; only unconditional and unconventional creativity, courage and care can captivate the curiosities of our women.

Bow. Breathe. Baila Bachata.

NOW. Bachata is the art of now.

*If you express your being in its truest form, in it's natural flow,
you will be rewarded immediately – not tomorrow but today,
here and now.*

- Osho

Persisting
In delay,
We are paralyzed
By the profound patterns
Of the past.

The past,
Provoking pain
And penetrating pleasure,
Persuading us
To permit
And perpetuate
The punishment of postponement.

Possessed by the past,
Floating in the future,
Thus profitless in the present.

Tussling
With the turmoil of tomorrow,
But tomorrow never comes.
Your tomorrow turns into
A replay
Of your torment of today.

*This is the real secret of life - to be completely engaged with
what you are doing in the here and now.*

- Alan Watts

We procrastinate and become pessimistic, polarized and
paralyzed in the present. Staying preoccupied in the past and
forecasting the future; the present becomes pointless and is
poisoned by prejudices and poverty. We are not available to
receive, respond or create in the moment. "This too shall
pass," but what if "this" returns? Do we just stiffen up, give up,

go cold or simply wait for the storm to pass while soaking in
sadness, misery and desperation in the present moment.

Those who procrastinate,
And take premature actions fail.

- Tao Te Ching

Burdened by the brain,
Our heads
Are always heavy –
Hardwired,
Hindered and hypothetical –
Hunting
For home,
Harmony and happiness,
But we remain negligent,
Neurotic
And narcissistic in the now.

*Making plans for the future is of use only to people who are
capable of living completely in the present.*

- Alan Watts

We pursue,
Ponder and pray
But remain puzzled,
And never positioned to propel
Above the predicaments
Of the past,
And into the promise
And poetry
Of the present.

*Internal debt,
Deeds undone,
Dreams unmet.*

You are perfection,
Now as you are.
The new
Can only happen
In the now.

Life isn't about waiting for the storm to pass. It's about learning to dance in the rain.

- Vivian Greene, Writer

In the present moment,
One simply participates
There is no need to pursue.

If not now, then when?

- Zen Proverb

Now is where we expand,
Nature is now,
Loving is now.
Dancing is now.
Happiness is now.
You are now.

The best time to plant a tree...was 20 years ago. The second best time is today.

- Chinese Proverb

Now
Is the translator
Of truth and transcendence.
We are tormented
By the tension
And tentativeness of tomorrow,
But tomorrow's triumph
Is triggered
By the totality of today;
By tenaciously
Tuning in to its terrains,
Temperatures,
Turning points
And treasures.

Only put off until tomorrow what you are willing to die having left undone.

- Pablo Picasso

Bachata Bond: We have become a culture of postponement. This is the basic premise of poverty, political propaganda and poison. We want everything now – excessively, expediently, exclusively - but fail and forget to be available and awake in the present. Now has become a nuisance - repelling the present by persisting in the past, taking punishment while the narrative and nourishment of now perishes. When our dreams, desires and deeds are delayed, we become desperate, distracted and easily deceived. The masses work and wait for five days, enduring misery, manipulation and madness at their jobs, before the relief of the weekend, only to marinate further in dissatisfaction, lack and loneliness. Happiness is always tomorrow - when I get this new job, then it's when I get the girl and then the car, the house; always something to ambitiously achieve and accumulate, to hope for. Our happiness is always held hostage. We are a nation of zombies, negligent of now and tormented by the drudgery of demeaning daily duties.

Patanjali, the father and founder of Yoga, states in his first sutra, "Now the discipline of Yoga." Now is expressed as a quality, a state of utter surrender and acceptance to *what is*, without layers – expectations, ego or external excitement. Be present and receive fully what is waiting for you. Do not escape for some superficial relief or disguise, as that only deepens our delay in all that we desire and dream. Never be numb to now, wake up.

Dancing is a total detachment from delaying, dwelling or deviating. Dancing is relaxing, receiving, responding and taking responsibility in the present, in the now. By dancing in the moment, you are spontaneous, alive, total and complete. Nothing more is needed.

What is now is undeniably new and this phenomenon of now and new is an absolute and natural necessity for a Bachatero to observe. Every dance is now, fully engaged, wholehearted and always new; never a repeat of old routines, never an imitation. The present is too precious to procrastinate or take for granted.

Bow. Breathe. Baila Bachata.

LOVING. We love by loving.

If you love a flower, don't pick it up. Because if you pick it up it dies and it ceases to be what you love. So if you love a flower, let it be. Love is not about possession. Love is about appreciation.

- Osho

Love will not lend itself to the limitations of logic, lust or libido. We cannot legitimatize love through the perversions of possessing people or lock ourselves in due to convenience, control, fear, jealousy, anger or insecurity. Osho reminds us that love is not a doing, it is a happening; it is a trust, not a technique.

Neither a lofty degree of intelligence nor imagination nor both together go to the making of genius. Love, love, love, that is the soul of genius.

- Wolfgang Amadeus Mozart, Austrian Composer

Love by letting go,
Evolve
From elementary explanations,
Words,
Techniques and advice.
Don't just look to learn
Or lean –
The ladder of love
Is not climbed with caution.

You know you're in love when you can't fall asleep because reality is finally better than your dreams.

- Dr. Seuss, Children's Author

Leap
Into love,
Into the unknown.
Maintain its mysteries,
Magic
And miracles,
Beyond the monotony
And misery
Of man-made meanings.

It is good to love many things, for therein lies the true strength, and whosoever loves much performs much, and can accomplish much, and what is done in love is well done.

- Vincent van Gogh

Most of us will only ever experience love on a localized level, usually through language. We say everyday, "I love you," just as much and monotonously as we say, "hello," "thank you," or "I'm hungry." We have taken love for granted and have reduced it to a casual concept. We can verbally mimic an impersonation of love but we will never truly experience or enter its essential essence. Loving is losing all labels, logic and lustful longing, one must get lost in the labyrinth of love to truly love. We experience love when we have become speechless, fallen into a sincere silence, and respond by renewing a deep relaxation into our romances. Love is flowing, formless and free, it cannot be fixed to any formulas, definitions or techniques. The quality and consciousness of love cannot be contained in any concept or conclusion.

If one loves, one need not have an ideology of love.

- Bruce Lee

Love is not a goal.
It's gifts
Are gathered
Along The Way -
In living,
Laughing,
And listening.

You don't love someone for their looks, or their clothes, or for their fancy car, but because they sing a song only you can hear.

- Oscar Wilde

Love by loving.
Love totally,
Wholeheartedly,
All-in
Or let go,
Don't be lame.

Love
Cannot be lukewarm,
Lingering in levels
Of laziness,
Lies
And liquor.

Unless it is mad, passionate, extraordinary love, it is a waste of time. There are too many mediocre things in life. Love should not be one of them.

- *Unknown*

At some point, the deepest love dissolves all formalities. Love becomes bliss that is beyond the body, words, explanations or descriptions. Love becomes formless. You can smell it, taste it, feel it and even drown in it, but you will not be able to physically or intellectually grasp it. That is when you know you have arrived.

I have decided to stick with love...hate is too great a burden to bear.

- *Martin Luther King*

The best things in life
Are not things.
They're not even thoughts.
They are that which
Throbs
In the thunderous
Thresholds of love.

Being deeply loved by someone gives you strength, while loving someone deeply gives you courage.

- *Lao Tzu*

Bachata Bond: We all lift the same weights, go on the same diets, watch the same television shows, eat and drink from the same restaurants and shop in the same stores. But the one thing that is sure to be different is the way we love and how we receive love, give love, look at love and express our gratitude and expectations towards love.

Most of us lack love, can't love, won't love, hate love and have never known love, so our experiences remain empty, detached, surface and insignificant. The roots of Bachata emanated from love; expanded, entertained and evolved through love and continues to express love. We know that we have arrived at the quality and experience of love, when we unveil an unconditional and utter acceptance within ourselves and share this awakening, abundantly and artistically, in all that we encounter and envision.

Love yourself first and everything else falls into line. You really have to love yourself to get anything done in this world.

- Lucille Ball, American Actress

Bow. Breathe. Baila Bachata.

ALL THE MOVEMENTS ALL THE WAY. As the Xing Yi Kung Fu proverb clearly states, "All the movements, all the way." This is the essence, intent and spirit of "Mind and Heart Boxing."

We are constantly compromising the consciousness and quality of our craft by doing things halfway – absent, aloof, asleep.

Pondering from the perimeter,
The peripheral,
Always partaking in partial,
Pseudo,
Surface and superficial pursuits -
Professionally,
Privately and artistically.

Endlessly enduring
The unforgiving,
Unsympathetic
And unapologetic wrath
Of unfulfilled dreams,
Unfinished tasks
And unattended visions.
Your world then becomes unfair,
Unbearable
And unnatural.

The greatest weariness comes from work not done.

- Eric Hoffer, American Writer

As Osho explains, "The misery in the world is not surprising; it is the natural outcome of living halfheartedly, doing everything only with one part of our being while the other part is resisting, opposing, fighting." Rarely, do we operate in totality – as a whole. Through this division, we are exhausted, weakened and afraid.

The hardships you harbor –
Hurried, heavy, hesitant –
Always halfway, halfhearted;
It is meaningless to do half,
Understand half
And be half.

63

Desperate and dabbling –
Divided, distracted, distant –
You've never written before,
You've only half written,
You've never painted before,
You've only half painted,
You've never trained before,
You've only half trained,
You've never loved before,
You've only half loved.

Fantasies to further the flesh
Into fame and fortune
Through fractional,
Fragmented
And flimsy efforts;
Forcing you to be frail,
Fruitless,
Flawed and forgotten.

Do not, under any circumstances, depend on a partial feeling.

> *- Miyamoto Musashi, Master Swordsman and Author of*
> *the Book of Five Rings*

Few follow through,
Finish
Or fulfill the fragrance
Of what they start;
Remaining fractional,
Foreign
And far
From our own freedom,
Fortune
And family.

Much of the stress that people feel doesn't come from having too much to do. It comes from not finishing what they've started.

> *- David Allen, American Author*

Be whole,
Wholehearted,
Complete and Total
In every movement,

64

Moment to moment.

Any man who can drive safely while kissing a pretty girl is simply not giving the kiss the attention it deserves.

- Albert Einstein

Bachata Bond: To be distracted, divided and detached while dancing Bachata is to be dead. To be split and not fully seduced by your partner or savoring the music and the moment is a sin. Finish all moves, moments, songs, celebrations – fully, totally, completely – and let it flow into the next, wholeheartedly.

Bow. Breathe. Baila Bachata.

FEAR. Be fearless! The common mantra of our time, but why should we be fearless?

Fear doesn't shut you down; it wakes you up.

- *Veronica Roth, Writer*

Fierce and flamboyant
But fictitious,
Fake
And forced.

We are trained and conditioned to be big, bold and brave; bulldozing our way through fear, weakness and adversity. We keep fear at a distance, failing to feel or free the fabric of true fearlessness.

Expose yourself to your deepest fear; after that, fear has no power, and the fear of freedom shrinks and vanishes. You are free.

- *Jim Morrison, American Singer / Songwriter*

Fear of the future,
Finances
And failure,
One becomes fenced in,
Fixed,
Not fluid.
Let tear free you,
Not freeze you.

Fear is not the foe,
Freezing is.

Frozen
At the forefront of freedom,
Fixated
On fabricating fairness in fallacies,
Fighting with friends as foes
And foes as friends.

The fragrance,
And the flowering of fearlessness
Is freeing fear into faith,

Focus and fortune.

A ship is safe in harbor, but that's not what ships are for.

- William G.T. Shedd, American Theologian

When we are fearless, we feel secure. Security is king in a dog-eat-dog, kill or be killed, survival of the strongest type world.

The science of survival,
Through force,
Grace or guile,
Scared with a smile,
Often suicidal.
The million masks
That we bear,
Only to fail
And falter to fear.

Feverish to further the flesh through form –
Riches,
Roles,
Ranks and reputation –
But we forgo the Formless,
Thus our fantasies are frail
And easily foiled.

Nothing in life is to be feared, it is only to be understood. Now is the time to understand more, so that we may fear less.

- Marie Curie, Polish Author

Flattering the feeble,
Sucking up to superiors and subordinates alike,
Securing status
And salary
But destroying dignity.

Osho teaches us that existence is all insecurity; that is all there is. Insecurity is an opening for our intelligence, intuition and instincts to innovate and influence. Intellect alone will not do. In society, security is sanity and insecurity is insanity but Osho believes the opposite is true.

Fear whispers wisdom into our will in the face of confusion, challenges and change. Welcome fear by letting go and listening.

Life is either a daring adventure or nothing. Security is mostly a superstition. It does not exist in Nature.

- Helen Keller

Bachata Bond: In Bachata, many dancers – students, teachers, performers - hide their fears behind the security of synchronized sequences, styles and choreography. This is limiting and imprisoning Bachata into a display not a dance; molding and mutilating it to fit your fixations and insecurities with image and ideology. This is bondage and ultimately becomes a burden to the body, brain and breath; breaching your bond with beauty and bliss.

Dancing is the art of flirting with fear, flying with it and freeing the internal flame that yearns to find its fortune. Allow your fears to flourish, to flower into existence.

Bow. Breathe. Baila Bachata.

LISTENING. Listening is the art of letting go.

The earth has music for those who listen.

- George Santayana, Philosopher

We live in a noisy world - often overwhelmed and overindulged in the superficial sounds, scandals and schemes of society; lured by lies, lust and labels. Loud and loaded, we are unfamiliar and unable to neither receive nor recognize the orchestra of the oceans, the whispers of waterfalls or the symphony of the skies.

As the famous Zen story goes, Master Nan-in was pouring tea in his visitor's cup. Pouring and pouring, allowing the cup to overflow, the visitor screamed for him to stop. "Like this cup," Nan-in said, "you are full of your own opinions and speculations. How can I show you Zen unless you first empty your cup?"

"Empty your cup" and unburden yourself of all self-imposing conflicts and complexities. Make room to receive, to listen, to laugh and to love.

The five tones are deafening.

- Tao Te Ching

The five tones – call, laugh, sing, cry, moan – is referenced here by Lao Tzu, in the *Tao Te Ching*, not as tones of truth but rather of torment; describing the distracting, destructive and deafening effects of daily noise - lies, gossip, rumors and violence. To prevent this poison from permeating the poetry of the present; one must find poise in the midst of noise. We often yearn to be heard but are too lost to listen.

A person does not hear sound only through the ears;
He hears sound through every pore of his body,
It permeates the entire being...
In that way the physical body recuperates
And becomes charged with new magnetism.

- Hazrat Inayat Khan, Sufi Mystic

Amplify the acoustics of awareness,
The symphony of silence,
Capture the continuous cadence
Of creative consciousness,
And synchronize
The sounds within the self.

Listening is a full body phenomenon. From earlobes to limbs,
fingers to feet, heel to heart, sole to soul, we must absorb the
audible and internalize the inaudible - savoring the subtleties
of both sound and silence.

"The sound of one hand clapping," is a famous Zen *koan*
(ko-ahn, is Japanese for stories or exercises used to enlighten)
that summons the "soundless sound." This is when one
transcends all sounds of Existence into pure spirit, becoming
an internal song that cannot be labeled, imprisoned or
controlled. The symphony of the "soundless sound" serenades
through silence.

Unlisten –
Listen without labeling,
Lessen logic
And the link to lectures,
Laws
And linear language.
Listen without judgment,
Justifying
Or juggling;
Just Joy.

The sound of rain needs no explanation.

- Zen Proverb

Loving is listening,
Laughing is listening,
Learning is listening,
Living is listening.

As Osho clearly states, "Prayer is listening." Talking is
meaningless. How can you advise and tell God, the Maker,
the Creator, the Heavens, what to do, how to do it and when
you want it done? Shouldn't he, she, they, it, already know?
Deep silence, awareness and openness are needed.

Preforming a prayer through language and speech, requesting what you believe to be entitled to and deserving, is often merely a display of desperation, desire and delusion.

Bachata Bond: The Universe is constantly communicating with us. Conversing through the narrative and nourishments of nature and always creatively questioning our spirit, sincerity and awareness. But we seldom savor the subtleties of its songs, we rarely listen because we are too contaminated, conditioned, closed and distracted by the decibels of society; obstructing our opportunities to listen to the lyrics of life through the eloquence of everyday expressions.

Bachata is the "soundless sound." The music, dance, spirit and culture are captured and carried internally, the beat is beyond the feet, the street or anywhere we meet. No radio, concert or excuse is needed to dance Bachata.

As a Bachatero, we hold in high regard, the responsibility to listen to our loved ones, our dance partner, our women. To fully listen, we must first let go of the need to judge, prove, interrupt or overpower so that we can effortlessly release every limitation that prevents us from being completely open and receptive to the messages of the moment. Bachata is the art of listening. Listening is being aware, alert and completely available in the present. Listening is the power to penetrate the potential and poetry of our women. In Bachata, we listen with our fingers, our eyes, bones, breath, heart and our entire body as a whole, totally and completely.

Bow. Breathe. Baila Bachata.

MEDITATING. Money has a monopoly on the minds, muscles, morals and motives of men.

Reading makes a full man – meditation makes a profound man.

- Benjamin Franklin

Money matters;
Mentality of the masses -
Mechanical,
Mediocre
And mindless.
Misusing muscle
To intimidate and manipulate,
Amassing meaningless material
To emulate
The magnificence of man.

The monstrosity of the modern man –
Molested by misery
And misinterpreting Machiavellian methods
To rule,
Reign and rape.
Monogamy means monotony
And mutilates to misogyny.

Aimlessly aggressive,
Arrogant
And unapologetic
For undervaluing the voice,
Vision
And value
Of our women.

Mentally mauled
By a million moods,
The modern man
Is a nauseating nightmare
Of narcissism,
Neurosis
And negligence.

Magnifying madness,
Malice
And mercilessly

Marinating
In materialistic monologues;
Seeking
Muse and meaning
In the mundane,
Merging mindlessly
Into the mannerisms of machines.

Mind over matter,
Methods to master the mind –
Modifying, molding, managing.
Marketplace mentality,
A magnet to disease,
Distractions
And destruction.
A total mutilation of mind;
Making a mess
Of masculinity.

The mind cannot penetrate meditation; where mind ends,
meditation begins.

- Osho

Society has formulated millions of methods and mechanisms
to manage the mind - motivating, measuring, mesmerizing –
through religions, affirmations, mantras, massage, magic and
medicine. There are so many techniques and trends to train,
tease and tame the mind; to program, control and condition
your thinking.

In meditation,
Vanity vanishes,
A witness awaits,
All masks are removed.

Meditation is marketed to the masses as therapy, "a thing to
do", an "esoteric exercise" to relax, be happy, overcome stress
and sleep better; a trance to temporally relieve tension. One is
often told to set aside a time to "do it," either in the morning
or at night or try your best to "fit it into your schedule."
Meditation is infested with interpretations that make it a
mystical secret, modern mental magic or a mechanism to
promote positivity. Informed but not transformed, we remain
imitative and immature.

Not merely concentrating,
Controlling
Or forcing
The mind to focus,
Relax,
Reflect and believe;
Meditation is mastery in the moment –
Alive, awakened, alert –
No matter morning or midnight,
Without monasteries,
Mountaintops
Or in temples in Tibet.

Meditation is meeting, melting and marbleizing with the immediate moment while remaining mindful and attentive to master the very next; an instantaneous internal illumination from moment to moment. As the Ancient Chinese Masters describe it, "Meditation is stillness in movement and movement in stillness." The Zen concept of "No Mind" depicts the quality of the meditative mind. "No Mind" is the unobstructed, uncontaminated, and unflinching mind. It does not carry any baggage, limitations or pre-determined distractions. Meditation is when morality arises effortlessly and mistakes are not merely mindless but meaningful. Painting is meditative, exercising, cooking, running, basketball and sex all are meditative and can transcend all mind and movements into the mystery, miracle and magic of the moment. Merge into meditation and witness your own self-worth, wisdom, warmth and wellness.

The mind marinates in a misty
And myopic
View of the world,
Thus everything is hard -
A struggle, a sacrifice, a scandal.

We continue to miss the moment with the mind.
Lessen the link to methods,
Rituals
And Routines.
Move past the material,
The money,
Mutilations and mediocrity.

March as men,
Meditate as masters,
Marbleize like moon.

Bachata Bond: Dancing with the mind is to be mechanical –
thinking, testing, trying – but the music has now internally
muted and the focus has shifted to the distractions, distinctions
and dictations of your mind. Your movements have now been
separated from the music and the moment. Your body is
moving but your soul and spirit are not. Your insecurities and
ideals are inflated but your intent is idle.

Bachata is meditative by nature; it is one of the most
meditative forms of art, dance, connection and love that
exists. To merge and melt into the music, the moment, and to
fully dissolve and disappear into the dance, is to be fully
present, engaged and free. You are no longer just dancing
from the surface; you are now savoring from the center.
Technique and timing have transcended to temperature and
truth. You are fully integrated – intimate, intense and
illuminated. With your ego and external efforts extinguished,
you will experience the totality of being instinctive, unscripted
and unburdened. This is when you will experience
meditation, no longer as a thing to do, but as pure presence
where the moment merges into the experience and
experiencer – the moment decides and delivers the dance.

Bow. Breathe. Baila Bachata.

SPONTANEITY. Spontaneity is the art of celebration and surprise. Living spontaneously is the spark that silences the debilitating systems, suggestions and status quo of society.

The humor of the heavens
And the hubris of man,
Hypnotized
By hierarchy
And hardened
By the hallucinations
Of habits and rituals.

Born and reborn into routines –
Repeating
And renewing roadblocks
And regrets.
Tactical,
And technical
But textbook and predictable,
Preventing the sounds,
Smells
And sights
Of spontaneity to surface.

I never made one of my discoveries through the process of rational thinking.

- Albert Einstein

Floyd Mayweather, Jr., arguably the greatest boxer and prizefighter that has ever lived and performed, is a sage of spontaneity. He revealed that he never studies videotapes or the past performances of upcoming opponents. He reminds us that everything can change at any given moment, especially on the night of a fight, so the highest levels of sensitivity and awareness must be available to adapt, relax and respond to the moment at hand. By being spontaneous and not forced or fixed to a pre-determined game plan, he can easily sense and adapt to all present possibilities and situations – danger, injury, advantages, weaknesses, mistakes, changes, pain – as he often repeats, "I always find a way to win."

Struggle and suffering subsides
When spontaneity sprouts,
Sings

And seduces your spirit.

Suspend the scripts,
Stories,
And statistics of society
And start savoring
Your own adventure,
Singing your own song.

Everything in the world is about sex except sex. Sex is about power.

- Oscar Wilde

Even sex
Has been subdued
And suppressed
By the stiffness of society.

The full spectrum of sex –
Erotic, climactic, poetic,
Orgasmic and romantic,
Has been reduced to regret
And repetition.
Erotic eloquence,
Excitement
And expansion
Has been substituted by
Self-satisfaction
And the predictability
Of personal pleasure,
Pride
And products.

Localized to limbs,
Lust
And lies;
Lingering in loneliness
And lacking love.

Spontaneity
Is not an absence of order
Or acting aimlessly,
Carelessly
Or violently.

Just think of the patterns of clouds,
Markings on a piece of jade
Or the prints on your palm.

Most live a double life,
Always split,
Stressed,
Jailed,
Jaded and judged at your job,
Lost in labor,
Lust,
Luxury and lies.

Passionate about painting
But settling as a salesman,
Serenading your sweetheart
But thinking of another,
Staring at screens –
Sleepy
Weak and wishing
For the will
And wisdom
To try something worthwhile.

Propel yourself,
From protocol to poetry,
Logic to love,
Judgment
And jealousy to joy and jazz,
This is the spark of spontaneity.

Life is a lot like jazz...it's best when you improvise.

- George Gershwin, American Composer and Pianist

Regrets of the rat race,
Rotting in the rigorous regimens
Of repetition.
We have the right
To reinvent
To renew
And reinvent all that is "reasonable,"
"Rational"
"Required" and "realistic."

Rebuild your own unique roadmap
And refrain
From ever returning
To the robotic rituals
Of society.
Now,
Relax and let it R.A.I.N.
R.A.I.N. = Ridiculous, Absurd, Irrational, Now.

All greatness includes at least a touch of madness.

- Aristotle

Can something new actually happen? Are greatness and
wealth really possible? Are the highest levels of health,
prosperity and success even available for people like me? Will
my ideas ever work? Has this ever even been done before?
How can I possibly make something like this work? Is this
within my reach or too big to even pursue? Let it R.A.I.N. and
let go. Get messy, get ugly, color outside the lines and break
through all bondages, burdens and self-defeating limitations to
unveil your deepest essence, emotions and expressions.

What was once ridiculous
And ridiculed is now right,
What was once absurd
Is now abundant and artistic,
What was once irrational
Is now influential.
These were all "impossibles"
And "nevers"
That inevitable turned into Now.

I am the greatest. I said that even before I knew I was.

- Muhammad Ali

Sazon
Is the superpower
Of spontaneity.

A superior synthesis
Of spontaneous spirit
And spice.
Never a technique

And cannot be taught,
This is the irreplaceable,
Inexhaustible
And often inexplicable ingredient
Of all internal illumination.

If I tell you I am good, probably you will say I'm boasting. But if I tell you I'm no good, you'll know I'm lying.

- Bruce Lee

Sazon (sah-sohn) is a term in Spanish used to describe "spice," originality or something special and unique. Sazon is a space, a song, a spirit deep inside that only you can understand, access and express. It is a switch that only you can turn on and off. Sazon is not merely contrived confidence or a fabricated personality; it is the very soul, the climax of creative consciousness for any awakened or artistic endeavor.

Each morning when I awake, I experience again the supreme pleasure – that of being Salvador Dali.

- Salvador Dali, Artist and Surrealist Painter

Sazon is the opposite of operating from a set schedule – daily, monthly, yearly, and even hourly – and succumbing to the stale standards of society. Sazon is the song that keeps on singing, whispering, changing, permeating, adapting, awakening, lifting, learning and healing.

If you look deeply into life, nouns start disappearing, and there are only verbs.

- Osho

The very essence of the Universe and the nature of humanity are embedded in verbs; continuous change - creating, celebrating, balancing, adapting, transitioning, evolving, opening and closing and contracting and expanding. Buddha did not believe in blind beliefs or behaving through the conclusions of others. He encouraged knowing, not knowledge. Knowledge is merely an accumulation and repetition of dead or outdated facts and information, rituals of ready-made religions and borrowed behavior. We continue to read and read, reciting recipes but never actually cooking.

Wander where there is no path.

- Chuang Tzu, Taoist Master and Lao Tzu's Disciple

Why am I always stuck doing the same things? Frustrated around the same people? Same results? Same routines? Stiff and stagnant? These are the questions of the servants, slaves, pawns and puppets of society. Only an awakened artist of life, a creator, a contributor, a soldier of spontaneity and sazon, can elevate above the zombies, robots and crowds of society. Spontaneity is the essence of the Tao. Osho calls the Tao the most dangerous path there is; unpaved, unpredictable, alive and unique to you. Every moment is a new mystery, a possibility for a new miracle.

If you even dream of beating me, you'd better wake up and apologize.

- Muhammad Ali

Bachata Bond: Spontaneity and sazon are the special sauces that stimulates and gives birth to new experiences in every aspect of life – dance, art, relationships, eating, cooking, travelling. These two ingredients cannot be taught through techniques or technology, nor can they be hardwired to your nervous system through years of robotic and rigid repetition of routines.

Zen teaches, "If you memorize slogans, you are unable to make subtle adaptations according to the situation." Do not succumb to the "slogans" of structure, stance and the standards of schools and systems. A spontaneous spirit soaked with sazon is the source of originality, sincerity to self, security within insecurity and insecurity within security. This is the formlessness of Bachata – free, fluid and fierce.

Bow. Breathe. Baila Bachata.

LANGUAGING. Release language from the limitations of labels, logic and law and allow it to leap into love.

Dance is the hidden language of the soul.

- Martha Graham, American Dancer

The significance of words,
Sacred
And soothing
But serves only as a starting point
For communication,
Integration
And truth.

Words become walls,
Worthless
And weakened
By the superficial speech
And slander
Of society;
Stuck and stuttering
In slang
And selfish slogans.

Lies,
Lust and lack lingers
As we latch on to the looks and labels
Of life,
Labor,
Luxury and love –
Lost in the lifeless lineage
Of lazy lingo.

The menu is not the meal.

- Alan Watts, Spiritual Teacher and Author

The masses are falsely fulfilled by just reading the menu. Informed but not transformed, ultimately, all the books, sacred scriptures, religious rituals, superstitions and the limitations of lazy language will starve you. As Alan Watts questioned, "how do you describe the color yellow?" or "tell me how salty tastes like?"

Osho says that you cannot teach someone "Buddha" but you can teach Buddhism. Buddhism is just language, a vague verbalization, interpretation and explanation of what cannot be taught. You can learn about Buddhism – pray, worship, hope – but you will never *be* Buddha. There will always be a gap. You can repeat and be a parrot but peace and illumination will be missed. That is why the Zen proverb states, "If you meet the Buddha on the road, kill him!" Statues, systems, scripts and secrets are not needed. We work hard to cultivate a cultural, creative and cosmic command of our language but often end up just living and looking through the limitations of what we have learned and lifelessly locked into.

I like you; your eyes are full of language.

- Anne Sexton, Letter to Anne Clarke, July 3, 1964.

The transmission
And translation
Of language,
Through lessons in literature
And lectures,
Learning through robotic repetition
And mundane memorization
Of concepts,
Codes
And characteristics.

Lessen the link to linguistics,
Mind,
Manuals and methodology –
Structure, syntax and speech –
And listen
For the language
Of the unspoken,
Unwritten
And unseen.

Silence is the language of god, all else is poor translation.

- Rumi, 13th Century Persian Poet

Language is alive,
Loyal to living,
Loving

And laughing.

Glory,
Growth
And greatness
Are gathered not in grammar
But in grasp.

Fluency and freedom
In any language
Are never captured
In conventional,
Commercial
Or careless concepts
But rather in gratefully gathering
A genuine grasp
Of the underlying feel,
Fabric
And fragrance of
The universal language.

The limits of my language means the limits of my world.

- Ludwig Wittgenstein, Australian-British Philosopher

Martial Arts is a form of language that is distinguished by all different types of styles, schools, systems, stories and secrets but as Bruce Lee famously said, "Under the sky, under the heavens, there is but one family." The underlying and universal language in every Martial Art is the unspoken language of respect, humility and peace. The universal language of all life is love. But Osho says that language is useless for love. People all over the world, in every language say, "I love you" but very few and rarely are those words authentic and truly felt, not just said.

The Tao that is named,
Is not the real Tao.

- Tao Te Ching

All language – esoteric, scientific, cultural, social, literary – points to truth and looks to reveal the realms of reality, reason and rhythm. But how can truth be reduced to explanations and descriptions through theory, religious inventions, fleeting trends and gimmicks? A transfer of information occurs, but transformation and transcendence remains elusive. Kabir, an ancient Indian mystic says, "I laugh when I hear that the fish in the water is thirsty." Truth is all around us but we remain thirsty, homeless when home is within us. Kabir reminds us that there are no labels, gestures, rituals, classifications or definitions that can bring us to truth other than from the wisdom and wealth of within.

To understand the currents of a river,
He who wishes to know the truth must enter the water.

- Nisargadatta, Indian Spiritual Teacher

What is this all about? How do I know? How do you know? How do you know that you know and I don't know? How do you know when you know? How would you know when I know that I know? And how would I know that you know when you know?

Food and clothing can go, but truth must not be lost.

- Zen Proverb

Truth is the triumph
Of who we naturally are,
Without tapping into
Or trusting
The testaments of others.

Translate
And transcend our internal terrains,
Our natural temple of treasures -
Tears,
Temperatures
And totality.

Testing truth from an "empty tank,"
We push past the temptations and torment
Of being tired –
Spiritually, mentally, emotionally –
To unveil our being -
Unashamed,
Undeterred
And unflinching.

Be truth,
And all the searching,
Striving and becoming stops.

Truth,
Always found in subtle simplicity,
Never complexity.

It is truth that liberates, not your effort to be free.

- *J. Krishnamurti, Spiritual Teacher*

Throw yourself
Into the thick and thin
And threaten the thresholds
Of theories,
Teachers,
Temples
And technology.

"That art thou" or "That which is" –
All merely terminology
That teases truth
But do not allow them
To terminate the tutelage
Of individual transcendence
Through inner truth.

Informed
But not transformed,
Truth
Cannot be localized to language
Or limited to logic
Labels
And law.
Only loyalty to listening,
Living,
Laughing
And loving
Can lead you to truth.

If you cannot find the truth right where you are, where else do
you expect to find it?

- *Dogen, Zen Master*

Bachata Bond: There are many dying languages in the world. Dead, because we go on repeating and recycling old routines, hardening in history, tormented in the trance of tradition, worshipping, studying and staring at statues, systems and scripts. Languaging is alive, spontaneous and constantly changing, adapting, responding and reinventing; always a verb, never a noun. Everything embodies a distinct language – food, music, artists, nature, fashion – but by staying stuck on the superficial study of scriptures, separation occurs and ultimately severs all possibilities of fluency, grasp and transcendence.

Dancing is in our DNA – social, psychological, sexual – and it permeates the purpose, passions and pain of people. It embodies the universal language of love and transcends all religious, racial and cultural barriers. A Chinese proverb reminds us that no one has ever become a great rider by only reading about horses. The only way to grasp the underlying language of Bachata – sazon, emotion, energy - is to dance, dance deeply, dissolve and disappear. Then the language of Bachata will be expressed and transcended through *you*, not by reading or repeating routines, studying and staring at statues, systems and scripts. Be the language, be Bachata, be truth.

Where words end off, Bachata takes over.

Bow. Breathe. Baila Bachata.

CONVERSING. Conversing is a lost art. Everything is continuously communicating, capturing, questioning, collaborating and contributing but we are too unconscious to listen, appreciate, receive or respond.

Each song of the bird, and each cloud floating in the sky, is something like a message, a coded message. You have to decode it, you have to look deep into it; you have to be silent and listen to the message.

- Osho

Contemporary conversation –
Clumsy,
Chaotic
And confrontational.

Disconnected
And disguised as dialogue
But ultimately
Molded into a monologue.
A self-fulfilling spectacle
Of selfish speaking,
A dominant display
Of dumbness.

Chest pounding,
Clamoring
To convey conviction
And control;
Aggressively,
Aimlessly
And arrogantly
Articulating the artificial,
Sugarcoating the superficial,
Ceaseless chatter,
Brainwashing banter.

Listen to many, speak to few.

- William Shakespeare

The simple sources
To special,
Subtle

And conscious conversation
Are captured
Through a communion of head,
Heart
And home;
Synchronized with humanity
And heaven.

A commitment to compassion,
Continuous creating,
Contributing
And celebrating
Are also all crucial and central
To conversing.

A continuous conversation like chess,
Internal finesse,
Creativity must confess.

The art of conversation lies in listening.

- Malcolm Forbes, Forbes Magazine

Dialogue is the art of deepening,
Deepening into a dance,
A back and forth, a coming together,
A celebration.

Like dining.

Dining,
Like dancing,
Is dialogue
And is distinctly devoted
To demonstrating
A daily deed
Devoid of digital distraction.

Our modern day dialogues have been delegated to devices.
There is a Zen teaching stating that studying a painting of rice
will not satisfy your hunger. Through screens and keyboards,
our dialogues are severely dimmed and superficial; serving
only as a substitute for conscious and creative conversation.

Cooking is a conversation;
Plating Poetry to your palette.
Teasing the tongue
With temperature,
Taste
And texture.

T-Bone,
Tapas and tequila,
Pairing tea
With tales of travel,
Wine with wonder,
Freeing the fabric,
Flavor
And fragrance of food
Through fire.

Chefs are conversing
With ingredients – deconstructing, discovering, rediscovering,
simplifying –
As ingredients serenade the chef
With smell
And seduction.

Transcending the treasures
On our tables,
Gratitude in gathering,
Our Queens in the kitchen,
Kings contributing,
Family,
Friends and farmers feasting.

Eating with hands,
Humor
And heart,
Not just teeth and throat.
Buttering your belly,
Every bite bridges the best
Of boiling,
Braising and baking
To the best of your being,
Bonding with body,
Breath
And blood.

Go to any bookstore and you will find that the Business and Self-help sections are both always busy and crowded with hopeless and helpless souls - searching, seeking and struggling to stumble upon some magical solution, slogan or secret to change and improve their lives. Frantically flipping through pages and pages of promises and flowery formulas to follow, we remain disappointed and desperate to find meaning and motivation. The Cooking section is where genuine consciousness, creativity, courage and compassion are housed. The study of ingredients and our awareness and appreciation towards them, mirrors the intimacy that we, as humanity, must hone. Finding the fire that unleashes the flavor and fragrance of all that fuels our families, fortunes and fitness is the art of sharing the temperatures, textures and tastes of truth.

Cooking and cuisine
Serves as a conduit
To Heaven and Earth, land and water,
Face to face with nature,
Conversing with color and climate,
Seeking and savoring the source -
Oceans, fields and forests,
Soil, seeds and seasons.

Our conversation with nature - appreciating and seeking the sources of our foods - has been muted and mutilated by the marriage of machines and mass production. Pre-packaged, pretentious and poisoned – locally and globally. An institution of chemicals and disguise, food has been reduced to numerical figures as we cautiously consume and count calories - unconscious, unappreciative and unaware. Food is no longer associated with freedom, hunger, necessity or nourishment but rather of waste, engineering, decadence and display. Drinking, devouring and digesting but disconnected from a direct dialogue with integrity, celebration and wellness.

From pigment to portions,
Flavor and fragrance,
To the sincerity of our stove,
Cuisine clarifies culture
And consciousness.
Always committed
To creative compassion
And courage,

Chopping away boundaries and barriers to serve all. Simple ingredients and recipes like simple speech and dialogue are the most effective, eloquent and eternal.

The ancient classics of Chinese cultivated conversations, clues, books and poems such as *The Tao Te Ching, I-Ching and The Art of War* - are still active, applicable and admirable today because it was a direct conversation with nature – man and woman, mountains and moon, sun, stars and sand; receiving and responding to the unchanging and ever-changing truth.

Bachata Bond: Bachata and breaking bread, the most beautiful and blissful combination, are both a continuous conversation complemented by compassion, creativity and courage. An eloquent back and forth, side to side, circling and relaxing into each other, the moment and the music; like a river flowing.

Our modern day dialogue reflects how most of us dance - a mere display of domination, distraction and desperation, mostly meaningless chatter and mindless movement, wasteful and aggressive; mirroring how most of us eat.

Chefs seek the source of their ingredients to intensify their interaction and integration with their environment and resources. A chef who is aware and appreciative of the source ascends into abundance and will never be malnourished or hurt by hunger – biologically or spiritually. Share, shake, speak and celebrate like a chef.

Be mindful of conversation. Whether through words, dancing or cooking, the quality of our interaction and reception can easily mean the difference between bride or breakup, deep or distant, golden brown or burnt, ready or rare. Even when we talk to ourselves, are we merely cold, cunning and convincing or desperate and destructive? We can either talk ourselves *into* something or completely out of it.

We are constantly communicating with our women – but how? What are we saying? What are we actually saying as opposed to what we wanted to say? More often than not, we are unclear, we stutter and succumb to surface connections. This leaves our women lost, alone, dissatisfied and unsupported. This is extremely common in dancing. Bachateros stick with simplicity and sincerity in speech and steps, never confused or consumed by the complexities of conventional conversation and maintains consciousness to caress her creativity and curiosities without compromise.

Bow. Breathe. Baila Bachata.

STRUGGLING. Constant struggling has become the very foundation of who we are, what we do and how we do it. We struggle internally, socially, financially, sexually, spiritually – always obstructing, overpowering and overlooking the openings to our own opportunities.

Struggle and sin,
Sacrifice and suffer,
Any means to win.

Under the spell of struggling,
We remain sterile,
Stagnant
And stiff.

Servants
To others sponsoring our success –
We are easily swayed
And often succumb
To the seduction of securing
Superficial status
And significance.

Souls stained,
Spirits shattered
And bodies blemished,
Always resisting,
Fatigued,
Fighting
And forcing.

Rather have a short life doing what you love than a long life spending it in a miserable way.

- Alan Watts

Stressed,
Strained and sleepless,
Always on the brink
Of financial crisis, spiritual confusion,
Emotional duress and social panic,
We continue to lack
And fail,
Becoming more angry,
Anxious,

Envious and violent.

Struggling with symbols,
Sex
And soul,
Tangled
In the tears
Of our temptations,
Soaking in sadness,
Sickness
And suicide.

Shackled
By self-sabotage;
Too spoiled,
Scattered,
And sleepy to succeed.

Suspend struggling and surrender.

Surrendering is NOT giving up,
Giving in or gassing out.
To surrender is to cease all separation,
Struggle
And stress
Within the self;
To abandon all associations
With the superficial standards
And superstitions
Of society
Along with all other similar sources
Of slavery.

Surrender
And ascend to total acceptance
And awareness
To what is actively
And artistically available,
Accessible
And audible in your adventure.

No longer resisting
But rather now relaxing,
Receiving
And rekindling a romance

With your own rhythms.
Enter, engage
And ease into the expressions
Of existence,
Enjoy them,
Do not escape from them.

The Art of War, written by Master Sun Tzu, well over two
thousand years ago, remains prominent and practical in every
category of contemporary conflict, competition and
consciousness. Master Sun simply states that winning on the
battlefield is not really skill. "Winning without fighting, this is
the highest skill."

How do we win without fighting? Succeed without struggling?

The Book of Balance and Harmony teaches, "Deep
knowledge of principle knows without seeing, strong practice
of the Way accomplishes without striving." It further states that
deep knowledge is to be aware of disturbance before
disturbance, to be aware of danger before danger, to be aware
of destruction before destruction, to be aware of calamity
before calamity.

Further to this, the *Tao Te Ching* teaches, "Plan for what is
difficult while it is easy, do what is great while it is small. The
most difficult things in the world must be done while they are
still easy, the greatest things in the world must be done while
they are still small. For this reason sages never do what is
great, and this is why they can achieve that greatness."
Success as a superior sage, a masterful man or a conscious
king, is captured in strategy, subtlety, surprise, Formlessness
and the Way. Mastering the minimal with the essential – one
accomplishes the most by doing the least. The *Art of War*
states that the skilled and superior warrior seeks victory first
before entering battle while the ignorant and inept go to battle
seeking victory.

*To sense and comprehend after action is not worthy of being
called comprehension. To accomplish after striving is not worthy
of being called accomplishment. To know after seeing is not
worthy of being called knowing. Indeed, to be able to do
something before it exists, sense something before it becomes
active, see something before it sprouts, are three abilities that
develop interdependently.*

By struggling you remain stuck, stressed, sidetracked and stepped on by the superficial superiors, subordinates and servants of society alike. We are plagued by the persuasions of society to approach everything head-on, brute force with brute force, strength against strength – big, brave and bold. Thus, this is a society of sickness – symptoms, ailments and afflictions. Working hard, long labor - unhealthy and unnatural - resulting in violence, sickness, depression and desperation. This is what the Ancient Chinese Sages called, "Hanging yourself without any rope."

When the ego interferes
In the rhythms of the process,
There is much doing!
But nothing is done.

- Tao Te Ching

The hypocrisy of your hustle,
Misusing muscle,
Get out of the way,
You are the hurdle.

As long as man stands in his own way, everything seems to be in his way, governments, society, and even the sun and moon and stars.

- *Henry David Thoreau, American Poet and Author*

Exhaust your ego and then eliminate it. Disappear and dissolve into the depths and details of your deeds, dialogues, desires and dreams. This is the art of silence and stillness.

Silence is not the absence of sound or not speaking. The symphony of silence simmers in both quietude and chaos. It is simply a space, a quality within the self that cannot be disturbed by ceaseless chatter or be enchanted by the efforts and expressions of the ego.

Within each of us, there is a silence, a silence as vast as the universe, and when we experience that silence, we remember who we are.

Stillness is not the absence of movement or just physically staying still. As the Ancient Chinese stated, "The stillness in stillness is not the real stillness; only when there is stillness in movement does the universal rhythm manifest." This is to say that the quality of meditation is in movement and movement in meditation. One should be able to experience this space or quality of stillness in our daily activities and interactions; acting and responding with tranquility, clarity and serenity of spirit.

To a mind that is still, the whole Universe surrenders.

- Lieh Tzu, Taoist Master

Whether an astute
Or ambitious apprentice,
Scholar or seeker,
Success
Is beyond struggling,
Stressing,
Suffering and sacrificing the sincerity of self.

This is the mutilation of the modern man – scared, scarce, submissive and asleep - salary superseding spirit, soul and sex. Suspend struggling and the superficial slavery of the self.

Bachata Bond: The nature of Bachata is free of struggling – effortless, spontaneous and dynamic. Each moment manifests into the next as each movement marbleizes into the next, all meeting and melting into the music. But we are taught, conditioned and mislead to believe that struggle, sacrifice, stress and hardship are inherent and necessary in our lives. We feel guilty when something is easy. We must work hard and exhaust ourselves to feel worthy of our aspirations, desires and goals.

Our muscles tear and break down before they grow, seeds must endure storms and mud before sprouting into a mighty oak and a million cells are constantly and relentlessly fighting, dying and regenerating within our bodies to enable our blood and organs to be healthy. These "struggles" and "battles" are the natural course of the Universe, the Tao. But our daily struggles are mainly superficial, not sincere. We work hard and sacrifice recreation and romance in hopes to obtain power, profit and position, only to accumulate artificial comfort, confidence and cash. When we struggle, we are separating ourselves from the utilities of the Universe. Endure the expressions and essence of life by allowing them to work through us. This requires a deep awakening, relaxation and silence. Cease struggling and start savoring.

Dancing is not struggling. You cannot struggle or bring your struggles to dance. In dancing, as in life, struggling makes you stiff, static and stale. A Bachatero dances and immediately begins to dissolve – disappearing into the dance while all insecurities, impurities and impulses are dropped; all ego is eliminated. Now the dance and the dancers are one and Bachata unfolds into pure fire, freedom and fragrance.

Bow. Breathe. Baila Bachata.

SECRETS. There are no secrets.

All it takes is all you got.

- Marc Davis, American Artist

We are obsessed with "secrets."

Secrets to attract,
Accumulate
And advance –
Searching
And salivating endlessly
For some exclusive system,
Slogan
Or speech
That will satisfy
And secure our significance,
Superiority,
Sanity and success.

All secrets – metaphysical, religious, sexual, financial –
anything to help us win, control and overpower, to succeed.

The secrets
And sutras of success are many –
Scientific, esoteric, artistic –
But ultimately,
All claims
And selling of secrets
Are forms of separation
Within society and the self.

We exhaust ourselves,
Endlessly
And elusively seeking some specialized
And supernatural,
Spiritual system,
Style
Or school,
Only to settle for a shadow;
A silhouette of success.
Success
Is always somewhere else,
Always tomorrow,

Solely for the selected few.

We are puzzled
By the patterns of prosperity
And the psychology of success,
Mystified
By money and material,
And ritualized
By the rhetoric of riches,
So we remain far from the soil,
The source of the self,
And remain unable to be
Seduced by the seasons,
Stars and seas.

*You, the richest person in the world, have been laboring and
struggling endlessly, not understanding that which you already
posses is all that you seek.*

- *The Lotus Sutra*

Avoid aimlessly,
Arrogantly and ambitiously
Seeking externally
What you already posses internally.
You are it!
Complete,
Total
And abundant,
As you are,
In this very moment.

So what is success?

Success is simply singing your song – undeterred, unflinching,
uninhibited. A song inside that only you can sing, synchronize
and share. This is the art of savoring life – spiritually,
psychologically and sexually.

Students,
Scholars and sages,
Singing the seeds of success
By staying close to the soil.
Guided
By the symphony of silence,

Stillness
And spontaneity –
The original source
Of Sounds,
Smells,
Spirit and space.

Through the search
And desire for secrets,
You are far away;
Separating
From your song.
Through Silence,
Stillness
And spontaneity,
You are close to home.
We must always act,
Love
And respond from home.

I come out of the dressing room. I have supreme confidence but I'm scared to death. I'm totally afraid. I'm afraid of everything. I'm afraid of losing. I'm afraid of being humiliated. But I was totally confident. The closer I get to the ring the more confidence I get. The closer, the more confidence I get. The closer, the more confidence I get. All through my training I've been afraid of this man. I thought this man might be capable of beating me. I've dreamed of him beating me. I always stayed afraid of him. The closer I get to the ring I'm more confident. Once I'm in the ring, I'm a God! No one can beat me.

- Mike Tyson, Boxing Hall of Famer and Former Heavyweight Champion of the World

Come close...even closer...closer.

Come home.
Home is not where
But *who*
You are.

Zen Buddhism simply states that,
All is always available
And accessible,
Nothing is hidden,

All is unveiled,
When you witness
The wealth,
Wisdom and warmth
From within.

Suspend and sever all sources of separation within the self. Search no more, as you already are all that which you have been seeking.

Bachata Bond: The blessings and beauty of Bachata, like life, are not concealed in any special or sacred secrets. There are no secrets. Systems, schools or styles selling secrets – more dogma, more gurus, more exclusive techniques – will not bring Bachata, nor success any closer to you. The dance is in the dance. Dance, and all that was intended for you will indeed be unveiled to illuminate you.

Bow. Breathe. Baila Bachata.

LYRICS. We all want to be heard and say what it is we want to say but do we actually have something to say?

Wise men speak because they have something to say;
Fools because they have to say something.

- Plato

The vitality,
Value,
And valor of your voice,
Rests not in volume,
But in virtue.

Your voice
Is validated through the nonverbal;
In the vibration
Of your veins,
The vigor of your vision
And a volcanic
Inner vocabulary
That is creative and conscious –
Not just confrontational.

Those who know do not speak;
Those who speak do not know.

- Tao Te Ching

We all have something to say, whether through a craft, occupation or relationship. We have something deep within ourselves that we yearn to express and let out into the world. Be it a skill, an idea, a song, slogan or symbol; we are constantly searching for eyes and ears to entertain, to convey and convince the validity of our voice, vision and voyage.

Most men lead lives of quiet desperation and go to the grave with the song still in them.

- Henry David Thoreau

Verbally vandalizing our value;
Our voice,
Often violent
And vociferous

But vague.

Victory vanishing,
Our voice vegetating
And repeatedly on the verge
Of void and vengeance.
Virgin
To the nonverbal,
Seeking validation
Through volume –
Vocal
But venomous.

You're like a dull old knife
That just ain't cuttin'
You're just talkin' a lot
And sayin nothing.

    - James Brown, Talkin' Loud and Sayin Nothing

Voices and visions that are virgin to the nonverbal defaults to speech, thought and actions that are violent, vindictive and dominant in decibel but deficient in depth.

People value violence as voice -
Attacking,
Overpowering,
Ignorant and mislead.
Desperate
In defining their destiny
But careless,
Aimless
And ultimately
Weak with words and will.

The loudest one in the room is the weakest one in the room.

    - Denzel Washington,
    playing Frank Lucas in American Gangster

It is easy to be cunning, overpowering, hateful and harmful with our methods and agendas for delivering speech but our opportunity to convey our deepest messages, lyrics and love, rests in our authenticity and artistry.

A bird doesn't sing because it has an answer, it sings because it has a song.

- Maya Angelou, African-American Author and Poet

My Song,
I must solidify,
Emotions in motion,
Even my guitar must cry.

From victim to victorious –
Unveil the vastness of your voice.
Vested in valor
And vulnerability,
Speaking volumes
Not through volume
Penetrating our planet
With the potency,
Purity
And poise of poetry,

Until the lion tells his story, history will always glorify the hunter.

- African Proverb

The Ancient Chinese referred words to "fingers pointing to the moon." If you focused on the finger, you will miss the marvels of the moon. As Osho explains, "Words are just my containers, the content inside the container is up to the individual." Words were often not necessary in ancient times; the wise were heard through silence, the unspoken.

The essence of speaking is in not speaking at all if you can convey the idea without uttering a single word. If you cannot, you should speak with a few wise and well-chosen words.

- Yamamoto Tsunetomo, Samurai

The Essential, the truth, was treasured, transmitted and transcended through the unspoken; nonverbal. Clues, messages and guidance emanated from the eloquence of everyday expressions, the nourishments of nature and artistic ascension.

There is a voice that doesn't use words. Listen.

- Rumi

Use words,
Not as walls
But as the whispers of your will.
Learn the lyrics,
Then let go
And allow love
To lead life,
Not the limitations
And labels
That we lock into.

Words do not make a man understand, it takes the man to understand the words.

- Chinese Proverb

Bachata Bond: The lyrics of Bachata are simple and deeply rooted in *sentimiento* – the endless enduring and expressing of our emotions and feelings. They penetrate the core of everything we crave and clarify our creative comprehension of love, loss and loneliness.

There is a lot of noise, nonsense and know-it-alls in the marketplace selling narrow-minded material – music, books, seminars, shows – and everyone is imposing their might, muscle and message. The masses are fighting, pushing and absolutely obsessed with infusing their influence, whether through a business, talent or even just as a cry for help. The loudest ones are indeed the weakest ones, shouting and screaming for attention, disrupting the lyrical landscape of love, energy and expression.

The voice of Vincent Van Gogh, master painter, neither vindictive nor violent; even though he did not sell even one of his paintings during his short lifetime. He continued to share the whispers of his will and wisdom through his work, whether anyone listened or not. Today, his voice speaks volumes and continues to inspire as we are finally able to comprehend and appreciate an artist that was way ahead of his time.

Bachata speaks louder than words.

- Franko

Bow. Breathe. Baila Bachata.

NATURE. Our neurosis to be known, artificially accepted, admired and adequate has caused us to be negligent and numb to nature.

Look deep into nature and you will understand everything.

- Albert Einstein

Everyday,
Everyone endeavors to emerge,
Excel
And evolve
Into the extraordinary
By emphasizing ego,
Excess,
Expediency and electronic efforts.

Occupied by occupation,
Obeying orders
And oppressed
By the office
And opinion of others.
Obsessed
With outdoing,
Outmuscling,
And outlasting opponents;
Orchestrating our own obstructions
And opposition.

The only opponent is ourselves.
Overlooking the Ordinary,
Continuing to obsess
Over objects
And outcomes of opulence.

The great mistake is to anticipate the outcome of the engagement;
you ought not to be thinking of whether it ends in victory or defeat.
Let nature take its course, and your tools will strike at the right
moment.

- Bruce Lee

The powerful narrative of nature
Is optimized through
The orchestra of the Ordinary,
The devil

Is in the details
But the omnipotent
Is in the Ordinary.

Everything in nature invites us constantly to be what we are.

- Gretel Ehrlich, American Writer and Poet

In nature,
Everything is a dance.
There is no greater dance than nature.

The most perfect actions echo the patterns found in nature.

- Morihei Ueshiba, Founder of Aikido

The total disregard, disconnect and negligence of nature,
along with our continued egotistical efforts to engineer the
energies and expressions of our environments, all contributes
to the current malicious movements and perversions to nature,
ultimately, causing extinction, endangerment and evil. We are
destructively deviating from nature - resisting, reversing,
contaminating, claiming, conquering – and not realizing how
this translates to the scarcity, torment and tragedy of all
humanity – food, health, love and overall quality of life.

*I would feel more optimistic about a bright future for man if he
spent less time proving that he can outwit Nature and more time
tasting her sweetness and respecting her seniority.*

- E.B. White, American Writer

Cowards
Continuously plotting to control,
Conquer
And contaminate nature
With perversions,
Mutilations
And reversals.

We must revert
And rekindle the Ordinary
To observe
And optimize our original orientation.
Desist
And decapitate all deviations,

Dilutions
And disguises.

The orchestra of the Ordinary -
The original,
The fundamental, the essential -
Is engulfed in the elegance
And extraordinary expressions
Of everyday.

Trees and stones will teach you what you cannot learn from
masters.

- Bernard of Clairvaux, French Abbot

The Ordinary is open and obvious,
But often omitted,
Obstructed
And overlooked.

Obsessing,
Overreaching,
Overthinking and overindulging
In outward orientation –
We operate from outside in
As opposed to inside out.
Therefore
We remain oblivious,
Obnoxiously oblivious,
Overtly and obscenely oblivious
To the Ordinary.

Don't just overlook what you can't see,
Can't just overcompensate
For what you can't claim.

Just observe the masses doing everyday activities. Watch them
closely in cafes, malls, streets, offices – eating, driving, talking,
walking. They are mostly oblivious to anything that is going
on around them – head down, headphones high, eyes blank,
floating, tuned-out, lost. They are disengaged and divided in
all daily activities - eating but reading a magazine, talking on
the phone but typing an email, taking a shower but unable to
enjoy with a thousand thoughts attacking. We are zoned out
in the noises of narcissism, desperation, greed and fear. We

are in the way and too unconscious to get out of the way.
Therefore, the masses remain inconsiderate, mindless and
mediocre – affecting the enjoyment and energy of others
everyday, in every way.

The opportunities of the Ordinary –
Orgasmic
And overflowing,
Heaven in plain sight -
Owls, oak and octopus,
Skies, soil and seas –
Staying open to its optimism,
Every obstacle and obstruction
Opens an opportunity.

*I teach nature. I teach you to be natural, absolutely natural,
unashamedly natural.*

- Osho

Do not be possessed
By what you do not posses,
Overcome
Your obsession with the outside -
Objects of opulence,
Opinions
And outcomes -
All is complete,
Whole
And total in the Ordinary;
Always available and accessible.

*Chop wood, carry water. Spring comes and the grass grows all
by itself.*

- Zen Proverb

Satori (sah-toree) is the Zen concept of simply returning to
one's Original Face, or the Original Mind. This is also referred
to as Enlightenment or Buddha Nature. Buddha, literally
means "Awakened" or Awakened One." As one awakens to
their natural state of mind - uncontaminated by human affairs,
cultures, prejudices, scriptures, cravings and worship – they
are able to accomplish and understand the beauty and
profoundness of Ordinary things with complete awareness,

attention and artistry. This is not easy to do. Think about it, when is your mind ever fully engaged in something without anxiety, neurosis, ego, laziness or with the past haunting you. *Satori* is not an intellectual achievement or an accumulation of more information, knowledge and techniques, but rather a deep surrender, a letting go of all concepts, systems and ideology. Our minds are so clouded and filled to the brim with garbage and distractions that we cannot experience joy in Ordinary things – waves crashing, birds chirping, making a bed, breathing.

Kabir is a 15th century Indian mystic, poet and father that Osho describes as "absolutely ordinary," as he found and enjoyed "natural and spontaneous ecstasy" as he describes it, in every eye-contact, handshake, relationship, child, flower and fruit. Kabir elegantly extracts the beauty in ordinary things in his poems that are hidden and harmed by the complexities that we carry and cultivate.

The original face has beauty, the original face has something of the divine. The original face has charisma. A carbon copy has nothing.

- Osho

Obey your original nature
By remaining uncontaminated,
Unclouded
And unaffected
By the superficial spectacles
Of society
And the influence of internal ignorance.

Whatever cannot obey itself is commanded. Such is the nature of living things.

- Nietzsche

Our oxygen is our opportunity
To observe and obtain
The Ordinary.
Most of us lose our oxygen
Way before our objectives are obtained.
We die.

Dying
At our desks,
Drowning
In the daily deeds
And dialogues
That dampens our days.
Delaying
And deviating
From our dreams and destiny,
Our dimples are destroyed.

There are no straight lines in nature. Everything is scribbly, wavy, wiggly and curved. From the veins in your body to the branches on a tree, all forms of nature are captured in spontaneous shapes, sizes and forms. But society continues to straighten us out, always seeking to box us in. Everything is a box. We live in a box, go home and stare into a box, we work in a box, and talk through boxed-shaped devices all day.

The Ordinary self,
Doing Ordinary things,
In the most extraordinary ways.
Optimizing our oxygen,
Through art,
Cooking, dancing,
Looking, laughing, loving and living.
No outsourcing,
Endlessly engaging and examining
The eloquence
Of everyday.

When you can observe oxygen as Ordinary,
And Ordinary as oxygen;
Then –
You will be extraordinary.

Obey the nature of things, and you will walk freely and undisturbed.

- Seng-Ts'an, Zen Master

Bachata Bond: The messages and nourishments of nature significantly contributed to the original building blocks of Taoism, Buddhism and Confucianism. These three treasures transcended and penetrated the poetry of life from all angles – personally, socially, psychologically, sexually and even towards warfare. By appreciating the daily ordinary miracles of nature – the sincerity of the sun, the chorus of birds, clouds communicating, whispers of the winds, love from leaves – we can embody, engage, express and evolve into enlightenment through the extraordinary of everyday.

Bachata is the art of nature. An Ordinary dance expressed in the most extraordinary ways. Beyond mere entertainment, Bachata is deeply rooted in the elegance of everyday. A spectacle is not needed; we dance, listen, sing and dream without appointments or approval.

Bachateros must maintain the nature of Bachata. Every expression and movement should mimic the fluidity, sincerity and spontaneity of the earth, skies, oceans, birds and flowers.

Bow. Breathe. Baila Bachata.

ENERGY. Energy has become a major commodity in our society. As the outer world batters and completely breaks us down, we are constantly seeking external means to replenish and increase our supply of energy to facilitate our busy lifestyles and ambitions.

If ya ain't got it in ya, ya can't blow it out.

- Louis Armstrong, American Jazz Trumpeter

The economics of energy –
More energy,
No energy,
Unlimited and never-ending energy.

Conditioned
And contaminated
By commodities and chemicals -
Caffeine, sugar, supplements –
And a myriad of motivational media
Marketing fantasies in fitness,
Fashion,
Fame and fortune.

Energizing the ego,
Evoking efforts
Enticed by external
Vanity,
Vice
And validation
But our endless chase
For energy remains exhaustive
And elusive.

Use the same amount of energy required to pull others down, to uplift yourself instead

- Kamil Ali, Guyanese Author

Fatigued,
Feeble
And never far from the furnace of failure,
Our energy is blocked.

Blockages,
Burdens
And baggage –
Energy stripped and stolen
From our very soul.
Battered,
Bruised
And burned out by the outer world -
Depleted, deficient, desperate –
We are constantly brutalizing
And bullying the body
While bargaining
With the brain.

Only left over energy and the scraps of our spirit are spared for family, friends, loving and laughing.

If the basic energy is not stabilized, the spirit is insecure.

- Liu Cao, Taoist Master

The Eastern elucidations of energy are expressed in both the eloquence of esoteric expressions and in the extraordinary elements of everyday evidence. The Ancient Chinese Sages have explored, examined and entered the elevated echelons of energy by nurturing *chi*. *Chi* (pronounced chee) is what the Ancient Chinese referred to as the vital life force that permeates and gives rise to all living things in the Universe. The embodiment and expression of chi is the underlying understanding, skill and phenomenon that promote power, vitality, longevity and spirit. Chi is cultivated, collected and channeled internally and externally by the integrated interactions and expressions of Yin and Yang along with the harmonizing of the Five Elements.

Embrace the Five Elements of nature – fire, water, earth, metal, wood – as they are the elite and enlightened educators of eternal energy.

The Five Elements corresponds to the five internal organs – heart, lungs, liver, kidneys, spleen – along with the cycles of the seasons, our health and our moods. Any imbalance, extremes or deficiencies within the Five Elements, internally or externally, can lead to illness and destruction.

117

The fusion, infusion and reversal of the Five Elements gave form to the Ancient Chinese Art of Feng Shui (pronounced fung shway). Feng (wind) Shui (water) is the art of observing, designing, adapting and interacting with our environment to fully embrace and enhance the essence of our surroundings. Feng Shui is applicable indoors as well as outdoors in offering cures, blessings, change and improvements. The Chinese observed that the basic layout of a room or space can mean the difference between sleepless, stressed and suicidal or serenity and prosperity. Feng Shui is especially important in our modern era of artificial environments of steel and cement, air-conditioned offices and chemically enhanced environments, as we often easily succumb to these impurities, resulting in sickness and disease. We must endlessly examine the energy of our environments.

Only those who can see the invisible can do the impossible.

- Frank L. Gaines, Mayor of Berkely California (1939-1943)

Most of us associate energy with finite and physical resources – food, exercise, chemicals, rest, visual stimulation. Our eyes and ears yearn to be enticed and stimulated by external excitement for motivation and inspiration. The Ancient Chinese, however, were influenced by the intercourse and integration of the Invisible, Infinite and Immeasurable. Most have never mingled with the mountains, the moon, never opened to the orchestra of the oceans or summoned the sweetness and symphony of the skies, seas sands or seasons – the narrative and nourishments of nature.

The temperatures of triumph,
The seasons of success,
The climate of creative consciousness,
All we must possess.

Master Sun Tzu advised, "Avoid keen energy, strike the slumping and receding." Morning energy is keen; acquired, aroused and amplified by aggression, attention and adrenaline. Midday is when energy starts to slump and the evening is when energy recedes, as soldiers start to think of going home. Therefore, the skilled warrior avoids keen energy and strikes the slumping and receding.

Whether we are energized, strong, creative or alert in morning or the exact opposite, productive and powerful at night, our energy patterns are predictable, pretentious and easily penetrated. Our energy patterns are plagued by pleasure, poverty and pain – and perpetually prone to perplexities.

Energy has to move, it cannot be static. Energy will move towards sex, or it will move towards hate but it cannot be still.

- Osho

Master Sun employed the idea of "potential energy" to capture the inherent advantages and disadvantages (good and bad), strengths, weaknesses, changes and dynamics of a particular predicament, location, formation, situation or moment. By establishing and exercising "potential energy," a victorious army is never exhausted and can summon and repeat these patterns of energies without dependence on diminishing fuel – food, water, shelter. We often have "off days," days that we are "not in the mood," "could care less," or "just out of it" but armies in the face of death did not have these luxuries. Therefore, the intelligent and strategic utilization of natural resources, rhythms and recipes were respected and reserved for versatility and victory.

It is well known and documented that master painter and sculptor, Michelangelo, created his masterpieces with barely any food, water or sleep. He did not exercise three times a week, incorporating yoga on the weekends and complementing that regimen with a healthy and balanced diet, eight hours of uninterrupted sleep, vitamins or a perfect ratio of working, playing and praying. So where did his source of energy originate from?

Bachata Bond: The Ancient Taoist Masters taught of obtaining and optimizing the Three Treasures – Vitality (desires), Energy (form), Spirit (Formless). Vitality gives rise to Energy and Vitality in Energy gives rise to Spirit, Spirit then rejoins the Essence of the Tao, or the Original Oneness. Accessing, stabilizing and unifying the Three Treasures through purity and tranquility, is to express the Infinite, Inexhaustible and Immeasurable. Therefore, Vitality, Energy and Spirit must be guarded and guided to prevent loss and leakage through the eyes, ears, nose and limbs.

The dissipation, depletion and evaporation of energy, according to Master Sun Tzu, are the result of holding onto forms for too long. This can include physical formations, mental, emotional or egotistical. This is usually the downfall of dancers; getting tired easily, loosing enthusiasm – physically, emotionally, mentally – as we fixate ourselves on falsities, fabricated forms and perceptions of ourselves and of others – insecurities, jealousy, and competition. Not rooted in a sincere source of energy.

Bachata is the expression of endless, enduring and eternal energy – emotionally, esoterically, spiritually, sexually. The love, laughter, limbs and lyrics of a Bachatero are never dependent on physical forms of energy or external motivation. Their energy is effortless. The fire burns internally.

Bow. Breathe. Baila Bachata.

SMILING. Smiling has become superficial, strained and scripted.

Beware of men's smiles, they bear daggers.

- Shakespeare, Macbeth

We exert too much effort to smile.
Fake,
Forced and fabricated.
Outwardly,
We express grace and gratitude
But inwardly,
Our smiles
Simmer in spite and hate.

Savor the sweetness,
Sincerity
And spontaneity of a smile.
Use it not in spite
Or as a tool
To deceive or keep score,
But rather as a gift,
To generously
And abundantly give away.

Don't cry because it's over, smile because it happened.

- Dr. Seuss, Children's Author

Bachata Bond: Bachata is naturally soaked in smiles and drowning in dimples, whether you are dancing, watching, listening or just enjoying a celebration. Guard the gift of smiles from deception and disguise.

Bow. Breathe. Baila Bachata.

POWER. The possession of power through the possession of people, percentages, profit and product is only partial to what we have been programmed to perceive as power. Those spending a lifetime pursuing power through possessions, ultimately, become powerless.

Mastering others is strength;
Mastering yourself is true power.

- Tao Te Ching

The popular and predictable
Prerequisites to power –
Physical attainment (overpowering, conquering, forcing),
Product,
Protocol and price (persuading and provoking
People to purchase),
And through the occupation
Of paper pushing pawns -
Posturing,
Pretending and posing their way to the
Pinnacle
Of profession and prominence.

The bravado of brutes –
Big, bad and bold,
Backstabbing,
Bragging
And bullying
With bats and banter,
Savages
Seeking satisfaction
In the spells and spoils of sabotage,
Violence
Pettiness and desperation.

If someone puts their hands on you make sure they never put their hands on anybody else again.

- Malcolm X

Power is a performance. It is often perceived, pursued and proclaimed directly and indirectly, through symbols, forms, formations, formality or the formless. By probing and penetrating personalities, passions and pursuits, those seeking

122

power or those already in power, can easily pressure, provoke or preoccupy our modern day peasants and pawns into patterns of perpetual poverty – causing the masses to be passive, predictable and persistent in taking premature or postponed actions.

Prisoners of power,
Paradise
And profit,
We are polarized
And plagued by panic and paranoia
As we venture to take over the world –
Perpetuating
Pessimistic patterns of perseverance
And persisting in pain
and punishment.

Taking punishment is not cool.

- Floyd Mayweather, Jr., World Champion Boxer

As Master Sun Tzu wisely states, "When you do battle, even if you are winning, if you continue for a long time it will dull your forces and blunt your edge. The important thing in a military operation is victory, not persistence. An army is like a fire, if you don't put it out, it will burn itself out." Even the commanding storms and forces of nature eventually subside for growth and renewal.

Poorly packaged in pretentious pride, positivity and prose; perseverance has plateaued the passions, promises and prized pursuits of the people. We lose our sanity and soul by sticking with jobs, businesses, goals, relationships and daily duties that disgust us, hoping that things will change or get better. A plethora of paths to power, prosperity, prominence and peace are abundantly available yet we persist in the path of punishment, brute strength, force versus force, destruction and dominance in a dog-eat-dog, doe-or-die world. Whether we are taking it, issuing it or plotting it, punishment permeates every element of our lives – socially, psychologically, professionally. Our relationships, workplaces and daily lives are plagued with punishment.

Why persist in the predictable? Why persist in pain and punishment? Why stay stuck in the superficial systems and standards of society that starve us?

Only the path paved in spiritual poverty
Will be compelled to rely
On ruthless ruling –
Punishing, rewarding and replacing
To control,
Conquer
And claim the minds,
Morals
And motives of Man;
Capitalizing
On crisis,
Collapse
And recurring poverty.

Plagued
By the pitfalls
Of power fabricated
By force;
We are a culture
Of phony physiques,
Artificial attire
And generic gestures –
Hard handshakes, superficial speech,
Pompous postures and gutless grins.
That which is possessed through force
Will always be challenged,
Compromised
And ultimately taken away.

The Prince, by Niccolo Machiavelli, is a popular and prominent manual detailing the many dimensions of studying and securing power. We should ponder *The Prince* but, ultimately, true power permeates our people, planets and places through consciousness, creativity and courage, not confrontation or capitalizing on fear, greed or love. Proceed on your path through peace and purity. Profit not as a prophet but as a poet, painter, and pioneer – a creator for the Universe – collaborating, contributing and celebrating.

The warrior is one who uses the pen and sword with equal skill.

- Miyomoto Musashi, The Book of Five Rings

Power through passion,
Politics
And personality;
We are pushed to be
Proficient and precise
To perform as pawns
And puppets –
Productive,
Professional
And polite.

The pulse of power
Is not planted in performance.
It is rooted
In the rhythms,
Romances
And riches of the unknown,
Unseen,
Unwritten and unspoken.

Coordinate your forces so that there is a minimum conflict and maximum effect. One uses four ounces to deflect four thousand pounds.

- I-Ching, The Book of Changes

At the age of 29, Siddhartha Gantama, later becoming Buddha, meaning "Awakened" or "Awakened One," journeyed into the unknown by leaving his aesthetic life of luxury, affluence, hedonism and comfort. Shielded by the palace his whole life, he was unfulfilled and unsatisfied with the placations of property, profit, pride and people at his service. He left, ran away, and journeyed into the villages where everyday ordinary people resided. He encountered the poor and sick for the first time and began his search for truth. As he famously sat and meditated under the Bodhi tree while extreme physical duress, starvation and exhaustion, he ultimately relaxed into enlightenment and devised the Four Noble Truths of Life and the Eightfold Path to end suffering.

Buddha possessed all the power that we hope, pursue and pray for on a daily basis. He had the power to purchase anything he desired or dreamed of, had the power to hire and fire people, travel, eat endlessly, live lavishly and soak in heavenly hedonism. That is why Osho encourages us to be ambitious, to seek, to accumulate, to strive and enrich the ego to the highest levels. Increase your possessions, your power, your riches and status. Only then, can you realize and truly renounce all worldly and material worship. Only then will you feel authentically unfulfilled and exhausted by all your empty efforts. It is in that moment, that you will reach the heights of heaven, heart and happiness.

To dance is to be out of yourself. Larger, more beautiful, more powerful. This is power, it is glory on earth and it is yours for the taking.

- Agnes De Mille, American Dancer

Pass up the palace
And be pampered no longer
By predictability,
And perishable power.
Baffled
By so many hitting bottom
Battling for the bottom line;
We must burn all bridges
To the burdens,
Barriers
And battles
That keep us broke
Bland and bitter.

You are not your possessions.
Pain,
Punishment
And the patterns of the past
Are not permanent partners
With your potential
In the present.

The day the power of love overrules the love of power, the world will know peace.

- Mahatma Ghandi

126

Bachata Bond: The powerless spend a lifetime pursuing power by worrying about work, percentages and prices; pushing paper and posturing for relevance and recognition. It is usually just a matter of time when these same people realize that time has passed them by and often find themselves, unfulfilled, unsatisfied and unable to find what they were looking for. All their pursuits towards power were merely perceived and perishable. A man of power never claims to be. He does not have to. There is nothing to prove, nothing to pretend about and nothing to posses.

Physical power is the lowest level yet most people still blindly follow this etiquette, even while dancing Bachata – overpowering, controlling, dictating. Muscles, hairstyles and shoes are egotistically emphasized more than the expression, emotion and elegance of Bachata. True power in Bachata and for the Bachatero, is effortlessly embedded in the poetry of the present moment. A Bachatero participates in the present with his partner and simply relaxes, receives and responds to her body, breath and beauty.

Bow. Breathe. Baila Bachata.

BEGINNER'S MIND. The Beginner's Mind is a continuous love affair with living - looking, listening, laughing, loving. Blooming with the beauty of basics and new beginnings in every moment.

In the beginner's mind there are many possibilities, but in the expert's there are few.

- D.T. Suzuki, Zen Master

The brilliance of body and brain,
Burdened
By blind beliefs
And borrowed behavior.
Trapped
And tormented by tensions
And templates,
Aggressive
But asleep,
Motivated but mislead,
Willing
But weak.

Burning bridges to bliss,
Beauty
And Buddha Nature;
A blatant betrayal
Of the Beginner's Mind -
Blind,
Bias and bitter
As we remain buried
In our own baggage.

The Beginner's Mind is a Zen concept that reminds us that we begin with a beautiful innocence, an intimate bond with beginnings and basics, caressing our curiosities and walking in wonder.

The Beginner's Mind is breached,
Contaminated
With casual,
Contrived
And common concepts.
Conditioned by complexity,
We accumulate more knowledge,

More answers, more beliefs,
But we are not alive,
Not awakened,
Only more aimless,
Asleep
And arrogant.

My painting is finished when I rejoin the first emotion that sparked it.

- Matisse, French Painter

Beginnings are a bond with basics,
A birth and rebirth of peace,
Purity
And potential.
A bridge to the boundless.
Indulge in the introduction
And re-introduction
Of our most intimate,
Intense
And illuminating ideas.

See the basic, embrace the unspoiled, lessen selfishness, diminish desire.

- Lao Tzu

Broaden your basics,
Beyond the burdens
And boredom of your brain.
From Buddha to boxing,
Beethoven
To Basquiat,
From judgment to joy,
Limitations
And lies to love,
Loneliness to laughter.
Break free
From all brainwashing
To bring a new and unique
Narrative to what you thought you knew.

Master Sun Tzu observed that victory in all direct and indirect
warfare rests on the versatility and variations of basic elements

– alternating, reversing, joining, changing. He states "There are but five musical notes, but these five give rise to more melodies that can ever be heard. There are but five colors (blue, yellow, red, white, black), but these five give rise to more hues that can ever be seen. There are but five flavors (sour, pungent, salty, sweet, bitter), but these five give rise to more flavors that can ever be tasted."

The basics often break down first –
The fundamental faculties
Of our forms and functions,
Body basics
Weakening and withering away,
Basic math,
Cooking,
Geography and grammar,
Lost and forgotten,
The butterflies to see our brides,
Buried.
The honeymoon
Harmed
And hurried,
By the hurdles
Of our hardened habits.

A pessimist is someone who has forgotten the joy of beginning.

- Marty Rubin, Author

At some point in our lives, we find ourselves learning to love again, walk again, speak again, feel again and find joy again. We revisit and bond with beginnings and basics for many reasons. Whether through disease, disorder or a dismantling of your deepest dreams and relationships, always maintain the beauty and bliss of Beginner's Mind and the basics will never be burdened, breached or buried.

There is a saying in Zen Buddhism that when one is young one "sees the mountain", when one grows to maturity one "loses sight of the mountain", and that later on, "one sees the mountain again." When one embodies the Beginner's Mind, you will never lose sight of the mountain.

Be careful in the beginning, and you have no trouble in the end.

- I-Ching (The Book of Changes)

Bachata Bond: Bachata, like life, is not an accumulation of answers, routines, techniques, beliefs and conclusions. Dancing Bachata is a new dance every time, a new song to celebrate to. Either bloom with the blessings of Bachata or stay buried in the bondages of your bodies and brains, the limitations of your lust. Same moves, same feelings, same place and same arrogance.

The beginnings and basics of Bachata brought upon social, cultural, economical and musical breakthroughs. Bring back the beauty of its early excitement, enthusiasm, emotion and eternal energy. The Masters of any craft have all developed a love affair with the Basics and Beginnings of what they do; flourishing flawlessly through fundamentals and effortlessly elevating into the enlightened expressions of existence. Michael Jordan, NBA Hall of Famer and one of the greatest athletes and artists the game of basketball has ever seen, used to wear a new pair of sneakers for every game. He said that he wanted to relive and experience the new smell, feel and joy of a new beginning every night. Dancing Bachata with a Beginner's Mind ensures seduction, surprise and spontaneity; a new experience every time. Awaken, and begin the beginnings of everything once again, over and over again.

Bow. Breathe. Baila Bachata.

TEACHERS AND TEACHING. Beyond terminology, templates and techniques, a true teacher transcends these tangibles into timeless transmissions of turning points, totality and truth.

Teachers open the door,
But you must enter by yourself.

- Chinese Proverb

We are enduring an exhaustive era of expensive and egotistical education, artificial advice and cookie-cutter classes. The masses are pummeled by a plethora of pretentious products, prose and pretenders promising power, prosperity and potential.

Acclaimed authors of attraction,
Gurus of greatness,
Mystics
And masters,
Captivating crowds
With compelling claims
Of cosmic clarity
And comprehension.

Selling secrets
And commodities to summon success,
Strength
And superiority,
Conveying crafty concepts
Of confidence,
Charisma
And
Concentration
To control
Commerce,
Contemporary conflict
And the human condition.

The pretenders –
Prophets, priests, politicians –
Perpetuating phony prose,
Persuading,
Prescribing and preaching
The pillars of prosperity,
Laws

And logic of love,
Life
And longevity.
Profiting
And imprisoning the masses
Through psychological
And social programming,
Prayer
And praise.

I cannot teach you; only help you to explore yourself. Nothing more.

- Bruce Lee

Telling tales of trials
And tribulations,
Teaching
Through testosterone
And tactless tendencies
To tame
And take.
Students
Are tied
And tangled in a trance
To desire more techniques,
Technology
And trust.

Teaching without words,
Performing without actions:
That is the Master's way.

- Tao Te Ching

The traits
And temperament of a true teacher –
Offering tools to travel;
Not trap.
Transcending tradition,
Timing
And technique
Into the tutelage
Of temperature,
Turning points,

Transformation and truth.

A good teacher must know the rules; a good pupil, the exceptions.

- Martin H. Fischer, Physician and Author

The Tao states that the teacher teaches without teaching and the only thing to learn is to unlearn. The teacher's only objective is to present to you, your authentic self. A disciple of Zen seeks his or her Master not to crave or lust for more information or techniques but only in hopes to obtain their Original Nature. This is achieved during *sanzen* (sahn-sen) or personal guidance, whereby the Master issues *koans* (ko-ahns) or stories and exercises, to evoke internal examination and emptiness. In Buddhism, the term *upaya* meaning "skillful means" is often used referring to the method a Master employs to enlighten a student, usually through the subtlety of silence, surprise or spontaneity.

Enter the tenacious and triumphant tutelage of Sifu Vingrove Thomas, Founder of the Six Harmony Martial Arts Academy.

True embodiment of the Eastern Engine,
His exclusive
And extraordinary expressions
Of energy,
Etiquette
And the elements
Undoubtedly and unconditionally
Epitomizes
Martial enlightenment.

By making an incision,
Cutting deep
Into an individual
To induce internal inquiry,
Intelligence
And intensity,
He unveils and unleashes
The inner terrains and treasures
Of our temple.

He awakens us to truth
And the totality
Of our true self,

Often by imposing
The paradoxes
And poetry of pain –
Physical, mental, emotional –
To penetrate
The pulse of our purpose,
Power
And potential.

A Michelangelo of movement,
A Picasso of pain,
His martial artistry is alive,
Abundant
And elegantly exemplified
Through empirical
And esoteric evidence,
Endless examination,
Ethics
And evolution.

Osho depicts the transmissions of the Tantra treatises between
the Indian gods, Shiva and Devi, not as dialogues between a
master and his disciple, but rather between two lovers. The
deeper teachings of the higher, the beyond, the unknowable,
can only be expressed through the language of love.

Serve the Sage with sincerity, simplicity and spirit.

Students
Enter with emptiness,
Eliminating excuses,
Ego
And envy
To endure the etiquette
Of martial arts.

Simple and spontaneous,
Relaxing,
Responding
And staying open
In the opportunity
To obtain his offerings.
Grateful
For his greatness
And the gifts

We gain.

Poor is the pupil that does not surpass his master.

- Leonardo da Vinci

Every student must surpass their teacher, as every child must surpass their parents; this is the way of evolution in environment, energy and expression.

When your perception only equals that of your teacher, you lessen the teacher's virtue by half. When your perception goes beyond the teacher, only then can you express the teacher's teaching.

- Zen Proverb

Harmonizing head,
Hand
And heart,
In communion
With Heaven and Earth,
He hones humble
And complete human beings,
As he awakens
And amplifies the artistic,
Academic,
And acoustic acumen
Of his apprentices.

Anyone observing sculpture by Michelangelo just "gets it;" its essence and energy permeates you; you are enlightened. A ten-step manual illustrating how he created it will not benefit you. Truth cannot be transferred through technique, terminology or templates. Sifu Thomas is a presence, not a preacher. Prose penetrates through persuasion; it needs to prove, to promote a personality, whereas, the purity of presence exudes eternity without ever exerting any effort. The sun shines without speaking. The eagle need not explain. The mastery of mountains manifests without manipulation.

Sifu Thomas
Is understood through the unknown,
The unspoken,
Unwritten and unseen,

Not just the mind,
Not just intellectual.

Minimize
Mechanical mimicking,
Less muscle,
Marbleize like the moon,
Spark like storms.

If they haven't learned, you haven't taught.

- *John Wooden, Legendary UCLA Basketball Coach*

Protecting
And perpetuating the poetry,
Principles
And process of his art -
Psychologically, spiritually, scientifically –
Not through economic efforts of excess
Or exploitation
But by magnifying his message
And remaining immortal
Through the value,
Virtue
And voice
Of his disciples.

Father figure,
Not just a facilitator
Of form and formality.
Supreme sage
And scholar of the source -
Soil, skies and seas –
And a champion of chi and change.
He is an awakened
And authentic artist,
All-in,
All the time.

Bachata Bond: Nature is the greatest teacher there is. All the timeless classics - *The Art of War, Tao Te Ching, I-Ching, The Heart, Lotus and Diamond Sutras* – were all seduced by the soil, seas, sand and stars. The mind, muscle, music and movement of men were all demystified by the million moods and manifestations of the moon and mountains.

Sifu Vingrove Thomas, (Sifu is pronounced *see-foo*, meaning "master" or "teacher" in Chinese) Founder of the Six Harmony Martial Arts Academy in New York City, has been the greatest embodiment of nature that I have had the pleasure of embracing in my life. He has enabled me to embody the Eastern Engine and extend this education and energy to permeate every element of my life.

Sifu Thomas is a rarity as we continue to endure an era of imitation, fleeting trends and superficial instruction. Unfortunately, dance schools are not excluded from this disastrous dynamic. Look around you and you will witness the diminishing qualities from the original essence of Bachata. Economics, not expression, energy or emotion, has become central to most schools and teachers. The spontaneity, spirit and sazon of Bachata have suffered while becoming more robotic, pretentious and predictable.

Choose your instructors and teachers wisely.

Bow. Breathe. Baila Bachata.

FLIRTING. Flirting is the art of inducing intimacy through inquiry.

This is the glory of man. He is very small, but bigger than the sky because something in him is unique – the inquiry. Even the vast sky is not so vast as man, because there may be an end to the sky, but there is no end to man's inquiry. It is an eternal pilgrimage – beginningless, endless.

- Osho

Conviction,
Consistency and clarity
Are the common characteristics of success,
But the subtlety,
Sincerity
And significance of questioning
Remains the ruler
To all success.

Judge a man by his questions rather than by his answers.

- Voltaire

Constantly in control,
Quick to quote,
And arrogant with answers
But too qualified to question.
Too cold
To caress curiosities,
Denouncing doubt –
Thus failing ferociously
Towards fulfilling our fantasies.

The very essence of our existence is to enjoy the exploration of our environment, emotions, energy and evolution.

Examine the equation to excellence,
Expansion,
Eternal energy
And enlightenment.
Insist on intense internal inquiry
To induce illumination,
Innovation
And integration.

We quit
Because we do not question.
We are easily influenced,
Injured
And infected
By our inability
To inquire.

But who is asking the question?

One who feels ideologically insecure, inadequate and lacking
in material and social status or one who is sinking fast and
deep into self-pity?

We have all soaked in a classroom, conference room, car or
cubicle, questioning our lives with pity and pettiness. Why is
this happening to me? How could this happen to me? What do
I need to say? To do? To think? Who or what must I worship to
make things better? Why are things always so unfair?

This is ignorance and irritation, not illuminating inquiry.

Inquire with innocence.
Ascend
Into a quality of awareness
And acceptance
And the echoes of your examinations
Will enable an effortless entry
Into existence.

Osho teaches that our inquiries, our questions towards nature,
relationships and existence should lead to a deepening of
awareness, not an accumulation of answers and cookie-cutter
conclusions. One should allow the mystery, miracle and
mysticism of existence to continuously awaken our wonder
and innocence. Existence continues to creatively question our
sincerity, authenticity and awareness but rarely do we receive
and respond.

Quietly questioning,
And deeply doubting,
We remain free from fixations,
Deepening our discoveries –
Creatively,
Spiritually and sexually.

Doubt everything. Find your own light.

- Buddha

Osho also reminds us that a Buddha already happened, Krishna, Lau Tzu or a Kabir already existed, they already visited. We can imitate and become dead followers of scriptures and rituals or we can design and redesign our own dimples, dreams, deeds and dialogues.

Your quest for quantity
Will undoubtedly lead to quitting,
But your quest to question
And conquer curiosities
Will undoubtedly
Lead to quality.

Bachata Bond: Dancing Bachata is the art of flirting with fear, flesh, fragrance and fantasies. Every dance is overflowing; open with new opportunities to express ecstasy, energy and emotion. Dancing is discovery, a deepening – not drowning into dead ends or doing the same things over and over again without intense inquiry. The dance is dead without doubt; without doubt there is no depth.

We are conditioned for casual and collective consent, carelessly agreeing and accepting what society has planned for us; totally asleep. We act, think and live through the conclusions of others, dead scriptures and superstitions along with repetitive rituals. Questioning is uncomfortable, it requires energy, evokes errors and often involves insecurity. It is much easier to accept pre-packaged, ready-made, cookie cutter conclusions from others.

We are fearful of freeing our fierceness, our fire. We do not dare to dance our dance or sing our song but we easily succumb to the superficial standards of society, settling for the security of schools, systems and studios. Enlightenment begins with endless examination of the status quo and disintegrating all dogma that distracts and obstructs our doorways to depth.

Bow. Breathe. Baila Bachata.

DIRECT DIALOGUE. A direct dialogue with our duties and daily doings undoubtedly delivers a distinctive yet diverse deepening of everyday experiences and expressions.

It is not the same to talk of bulls,
as to be in the bullring.

- Spanish Proverb

A direct dialogue, or what the teaching of Zen refers to as "Direct Pointing" was a discipline that revealed one's Original Nature or Oneness in our speech, thoughts and actions without the influence or restrictions of any special doctrines, techniques or philosophies. Direct pointing is a quality of consciousness to help free oneself from all fixations and falsities of the ego.

The days of direct dialogue
Are diminishing daily.
Dreams,
Deeds and desires
Are distracted
And divided
By the screens of technology.

Layers and layers
Of curtains covering
And killing our creative consciousness;
Electronic ego
And efforts,
Erasing the elegance of enlightened engagement,
All substitutes – surface, pseudo, superficial –
Sacrificing sincerity and simplicity,
Deviating from directness.

Rare
Is a written letter, a note,
As pens
And penmanship are replaced by keys.
Care
And cordiality
Are communicated digitally,
A meeting of monitors,
Not hearts.

Electronic pictures of Mom,
Dad and Sis,
Artificial affection accrued
And applied,
But cold as the arctic –
Always a device dividing
The dignity of directness.

The Ancient Chinese Sages cultivated classics such as *The Tao Te Ching, I-Ching* and *The Art of War,* thousands of years ago and they are all still presently available, applicable and admirable because it was a direct dialogue, a direct connection with nature – man, woman, mountains, moon, sun, stars, soil and sand. The arts, mainly what the Ancient Chinese referred to as the Five Excellences – poetry, painting, calligraphy, medicine and tai chi – were vehicles to cultivate and calibrate a collection of special skills. These skills were used to stimulate and satisfy the full spectrum of our natural senses while securing the sensitivity of stillness and silence. Tai Chi (pronounced tai-chee), often referred to as the "Supreme Ultimate," is the ancient Chinese internal martial art that expresses the energies of Yin (soft) and Yang (hard) in movement, breathing and awareness to promote power, health and longevity. Masters of the Five Excellences were able to transcend the temptations, distractions, deceptions and diseases that contaminated our natural connections to existence – environment, energy and emotions.

The plays and poetry of William Shakespeare were also direct dialogues into the heart of human nature – pursuits of power, jealousy, and love. Lessons in life, love, loss and lamentation are still learned through his literature today as they continue to reveal the depths of humanity and our own deepest, darkest and most decadent desires.

The brush reveals what the tongue cannot.

- Franko

Directness
Is our opportunity to observe
And obtain
The deepest dimensions
Of who we are,
What we do

And why?

GO DEEP...DEEPER.....EVEN DEEPER.

On the surface of an ocean, you may only notice the constant crashing, colliding and restlessness of waves, but the true orchestra of the ocean lay deep beneath the surface of waves and into the depths of silence, serenity and stillness. Deep into the ocean is where struggle, conflict and collision dissipate and a direct experience with life, beauty and energy unravels.

Champions are made from something they have deep inside them, a desire, a dream, a vision. They have to have last minute stamina, they have to be a little faster, they have to have skill and the will. But the will must be stronger than the skill.

- Muhammad Ali

Dancing is deep discovery.

Dancing
Is not merely a display
Or desire
To dazzle,
Dominate or dictate.

More than a medium of movement to music,
Dancing is a quality of directness
That develops a database of depth;
Defending
Against distortion,
And disguise.
Dare to deepen,
Dissolve
And discover.

*Go deep, deeper,
Deep until you dare,
Dare to dance, dare to die,
Tao is to do, not try.*

Think lightly of yourself and deeply of the world.

- Miyamoto Musashi, Japanese Swordsman

Bachata Bond: The Ancient Chinese Sages ascended to the awareness that direct doing or "pointing" enabled experiences that transcended the limitations of language, mind, and ego. This emphasis on direct doing extracted the natural energy, enthusiasm, simplicity and spontaneity in every engagement; denying all doctrines, duality, theories and speculation. A beautiful Zen proverb states, "In walking, just walk. In sitting, just sit. Above all, do not wobble." This simple yet penetrating proverb pinpoints the essence of engaging all endeavors by being completely present, undivided and sincere. How often are we eating but thinking about work, painting but thinking about tomorrow, dancing but thinking about how well we are doing, listening but dreaming about sex? We are never fully engaged in what we are doing thus always "wobbling" and compromising a complete and direct experience.

Bachata is a direct dialogue. It must be felt, experienced and appreciated firsthand devoid of devices, deception or disguises. We cannot learn or love Bachata through videos or books, which would only be partial engagement. To dance Bachata is to deepen, dissolve and completely die in the dance, let go, surrender and from there, a direct and sincere experience erupts.

Bow. Breathe. Baila Bachata.

BELLY / WAIST / HIPS: The proof is in the pudding but bliss is in the belly.

Emptying the mind and filling the belly.

- I-Ching, The book of Changes

The belly area, or what the Chinese refer to as *dantien* (don tee-yen), is the foundation and center of wisdom, health, intuition, power and connection. The understanding and use of the dan tien are both critical to the spiritual, practical and philosophical development of the arts – healing, literary and internal Martial Arts including Tai Chi, Xing Yi and Bua Gua. We engage the power, information and truth of our dantien by sinking, storing, circulating and channeling our chi through the expressions and etiquette of emptiness and fullness, opening and closing and contracting and expanding.

Winning and losing is not a matter of book learning; it is a matter of how much belly you have.

- Master Awa Kenzo, Zen in the Art of Archery

The beat is in the belly,
Wisdom
And wonder in the waist,
Heaven
Is in the harmony of hips –
Relaxed,
Open,
Flexible and free;
This is the center of our soul,
Spirit and sazon.

Martha Graham, the great American dancer and choreographer, referred the torso to "the house of the pelvic truth" as she believed that the most expressive part of the human body came from the contractions of the diaphragm and the distinct movements of the torso. She emphasized exercises to express and feel the deep emotions and experience emerging from these muscles. The Japanese have a term *"hara gei"* (hara = belly and gei = art) meaning the art of the belly or gut. Hara gei was used by the Japanese to communicate, calculate and interpret everything from the timing and intent of others to cultivating calm, honesty and truth within oneself.

> The five colors blind the eye.
> Therefore the Sage
> Takes care of the belly,
> Not the eye.

> - Tao Te Ching

Banish the brain,
And beckon the belly.
Your bread and butter
To bond with your body.

You don't need a partner when you hear bachata. Dancing with your hand over your stomach is the solution.

> *- Bachata Proverb*

Bachata Bond: The belly is the brain of a Bachatero. We laugh, cry, dance, act, think, paint, sing, feel and breathe from the belly. Have you ever danced Bachata blindfolded? Try and experience the mystery, miracle and magic of your belly.

Bow. Breathe. Baila Bachata.

ACTION. We are obsessed with "being busy," always "doing something," short on time and occupied with anything and everything. But what are we really doing?

If there's a book you really want to read, but it hasn't been written yet, then you must write it.

- Toni Morrison, American Novelist

Billions born,
But few are alive,
Awake
Or aware,
And even fewer
Answer the call –
The call to create,
Collaborate
And contribute
To our Universe.

It is nothing to die. It's an awful thing never to have lived.

- Victor Hugo, French Poet

The ailments and afflictions
Of the average
And asleep;
Anchored by aimless,
And arrogant activity.
Awestruck
By the allure
Of accumulating accolades,
Advantages,
Accessories and answers,
Hoping to attain artificial approval,
Admiration
And authority.

The addiction to ambition,
The adrenaline
To achieve and advance,
Aggressive
But absent,
Fierce and flamboyant
But fictitious,

Absently accruing
Ambiguous appraisals
Of affluence,
Acumen
And abundance.

Don't write a check with your mouth that your ass can't cash.

- Anonymous

We ambitiously seek to acquire the answers, methods and
secrets to amplify our abilities and enhance our experiences
and way of life but we often descend deeper into despair and
desperation as we continue to deviate from authentic action.
We are accustomed to activity, often staying busy and
depleting energy on artificial aspirations that are not aligned
and, ultimately, against our own voice and values. Aggression
arises, as you continue to comply and carry out the agendas of
society, doing deeds to fulfill the demands and expectations of
others. Aggression is our answer, our asset to assist in every
encounter and endeavor. We eat aggressively, speak and drive
aggressively, becoming animalistic and abandoning all
awareness, artistry and ascension.

Don't mistake activity with achievement.

- John Wooden

Arrogance and aggression,
Articulated through the armor
Of automobiles,
Drunk in abusive attitudes –
Racing, raging, crashing -
Swerving deeper
Into ignorance,
Destruction
And suicide.

*The world will not be destroyed by those who do evil, but by
those who watch them without doing anything.*

- Albert Einstein

Be absolutely allergic
To the artificial armor
Of being average,

Arrogant
And aimless.
Artistically
And attentively ambush
And assassinate
All artificial aggression;
Dropping all deeds
Devoid of dignity,
Devotion
And divinity.

Nature does nothing uselessly.

- Aristotle, Philosopher

Action is an awakening.
It is the art of artistically accepting,
Adapting
And attending
To what is abundantly available
And accessible.

Be great in act, as you have been in thought.

- William Shakespeare

Ascend to the awareness
That you have already arrived.
There is no where to go;
You are all that you seek.
Abandon attachments,
Anxiety,
Animosity
And all the artificial assessments
Of society –
Deeming you incomplete,
Inadequate
And incompetent.

Be – don't become.

- Buddha

STOP AUDITIONING AND START ACTING.

Cease chasing,
Coercing and convincing people
To cosign your craft.
In authentic and artistic action –
You are accountable.
In aimless and arrogant activity,
There is only blame.

If you know your being, there is no question on becoming. All
that you have imagined to become you already are. You are gods
who have forgotten who they are.

- Osho

The awakened artist,
Acts and achieves
Without answering to artificial authority,
Never waiting
For the approval of others;
Not only self-actualizing
But self-authorizing,

Keep seeking approval,
And you will be chained.

- Tao Te Ching

Action is alive,
Immediate,
Spontaneous
And responsive to the moment.
Applied through the audacity of awareness,
Not accumulated answers,
Advice, theories,
Knowledge, doctrines
Or cookie-cutter conclusions of crowds.

Don't be satisfied with stories, how things have gone with others.
Unfold your own myth.

- Rumi

Great discoveries, breakthrough ideas and achievements were
all an attainment of awareness long before an answer.
Through the accumulation of ready-made answers –

academically, traditionally, religiously - our actions are automatic, artificial, pre-packaged and borrowed. Action must arise from awareness, internal intelligence and intimacy in the moment, not from answers that are rooted in the patterns of the past. Studies must transcend into spontaneous skill that seduces and penetrates the purpose, potential and promise of the present.

Pray to God.....but keep hammering away.

- Baltasar Gracian, Spanish Philosopher

The arousal
And ascension of your actions,
Amplified
By the acoustics
And aroma of skill,
Seduced
By the ancestry of alchemy,
Astrology,
Archetypes and the application
Of angles
And academic acumen.

Awaken to the anatomy of your actions.

Adapt what is useful, reject what is useless, and add what is specifically your own.

- Bruce Lee

Skills pays the bills,
But how is skill secured?
What are the signals
And symbols
That summons and relates to skill?

Skill and spontaneity,
Skill and study,
Skill and soul,
Skill and selfishness,
Skill and sadness,
Skill and stress,
Skill and strategy,
Skill and solitude,

Skill and seriousness,
Skill and street smart,
Skill and school smart,
Skill and sleep,
Skill and society,
Skill and survival,
Skill and seasons,
Skill and simplicity.

Skill and smell. Boxing legend, Floyd Mayweather, Jr.,
revealed that he loves the smell of his leather boxing gloves.
He attributes this appreciation as one of the main reasons for
his high aptitude, enthusiasm and effortlessness to his craft.
Statistics and studies show that for most people, their sense of
smell has either completely vanished or is dissipating at a
rapid pace. The loss of smell adversely affects and alters the
expressions, energy and enjoyment of what we do. Secure
your sensitivity to smell and all the other signals to summon,
satisfy and seduce your skills.

Skill
Is beyond the realms
Of reason
And reality.
Skill simmers
In the subtle space
Of stillness and silence
And is activated
Through the appearances
Of adversity and anger.

Sweet are the uses of adversity.

- Shakespeare

As Osho wisely reminds us, "When one is angry, be angry
totally, then there is authenticity and truth." Anger associated
with aimless aggression and arrogance leads to abuse,
violence and disorder. Anger accompanied by awareness,
audacity and abundance ascends to artistry.

Awaken to the artistry
And acrobatics
Of adversity and anger.

You can tell the greatness of a man by what makes him angry.

- Abraham Lincoln

Articulating action,
Through the analogy of archery.
The archer "shoots without shooting,"
Hitting the bulls-eye without intervention of "I,"
By aiming with the accuracy of the abdomen,
The truth hits the target,
Not technique,
Terminology
Or technology.

Dissolve the distance
Between doing and being;
The distance between dancing and being a dance.
From reading, thinking or practicing it
To realizing you *are* it.

In *Zen and the Art of Archery*, author Eugen Herrigel recounts
his study of *kyudo* (kee-u-doe), the Art of the Japanese Bow or
Archery, under Master Awa Kenzo. Archery was presented to
him by Master Kenzo, as a dance, spontaneous and effortless,
letting the shot "fall from the archer like a ripe fruit." Master
Kenzo stated that the bow, arrow and art are one,
transcending all dualities between the shooter and the shot as
well as emphasizing the philosophical expression of archery -
excellence in execution emanating from spirit, nature, truth,
breath and belly. Through this approach, Master Kenzo stated
that each shot or release reveals one's true nature and shows
what you have suffered through and practiced.

Less and less do you need to force things,
Until finally you arrive at non-action.
By not doing,
Everything is done.

- Tao Te Ching

Lao Tzu does not advocate the avoidance or absence of action
but rather the elimination of the ego – jealousy, anxiety,
greed, pettiness – to prohibit any possibilities of influencing
and interfering with our actions. His concept of "non-action"
does not promote passiveness, inaction or laziness but rather

the highest level of action; that is acting in accord with the nature of all things – relaxed, spontaneous, alive. The Chinese use the term "the uncarved block," to describe a finished sculpture and how the artist did not have to strive to sculpt it but rather simply allowed and assisted it to naturally be what it wanted to be. This mirrors the sentiments of Michelangelo when he famously expressed seeing the angel in his marble block and setting it free. This is the art of action through awareness, artistry and acceptance - not dependence, manipulation or force.

There is a vitality, a life force, an energy, a quickening that is translated through you into action, and because there is only one of you in all time, this expression is unique. And if you block it, it will never exist through any other medium and will be lost.

- Martha Graham

Abort all associations
With abrupt,
Abstract
And abusive activities.
Stop abandoning what is available,
Accessible
And abundant.

Mourning every morning
About miniscule,
Mindless
And meaningless matters;
Affecting the masses with mediocrity.
Wake up,
Not with an alarm clock,
But awaken
With the attitude
Of all-in,
All the way,
All the time.

Every man is guilty of the good he did not do.

- Voltaire

Bachata Bond: From armies and artists to the analogies of Nature – subtle, simple and strategic action has been at the forefront of all Ancient Chinese thought, theories, concepts and studies. From the prosperity of acting in accord with the nourishments of nature to the misfortunes of mistiming and misjudging – action for the Taoist Master was not confined to clocks, calendars and computers but rather in the appropriate awareness and adaptions to the changes in all situations, moment to moment.

Bachata is action - an awakened, artistic and authentic appetite for artistry. It is a hunger honed by humility, harmony and heart. It is not merely a pretentious performance of pointless pumping and ferocious flapping of your body. Adamant about being the alpha, the leader, the male dancer manhandles his partner but misses the magic in each movement and is merely mindless in each moment; miniscule in both mind and masculinity. Artistic ascension does not associate with artificial approval, applause or admiration. Eliminate ego and allow the dance to dance itself.

Bow. Breathe. Baila Bachata.

STEPS. Our steps along the way – small steps, big steps, missteps, sidesteps, back steps, a step up, a step down...

All know the way, but few walk it.

> *- Bodhidharma, Buddhist Monk*

Dig deep
And discover the
Depths of your daily deeds,
Dialogues
And desires.
Dissolve into the details
Of your defeats,
Dependencies
Distractions and disappointments.
Dance with them.
Let them speak.
Understand them.

Monsters are real, and ghosts are real too. They live inside us, and sometimes, they win.

> *- Stephen King, American Author*

Now,
Dare to depart from them.
Decapitate
The demons
That have dictated
The demise
And destruction of your dreams,
Dimples
And destiny.
Dispose of the drama
That has depleted
Your drive;
The drama
That has dragged you
Into desperation
And darkness.

May you live every day of your life.

> *- Jonathan Swift, Anglo-Irish Poet*

Each day, like dance, is composed of steps. Steps to secure a skill, a superior psychological state of mind, spirit, serenity or success. But what are these steps? Where are they taking us? Why are we taking these steps? What do they mean? Do they even matter? Am I wasting my time? Can I trust my steps? Do I continue?

When you dance, your purpose is not to get to a certain place on the floor. It's to enjoy each step along the way.

- Wayne Dyer, American Self-Help Author

Each single step
Grants either
A gap or a gift,
And within each gap
Is a gift
And in each gift,
A gap.

The artist is nothing without the gift, but the gift is nothing without the work.

- Emile Zola, French Writer

What is this gap that we cannot grasp? What is this elusive space that seems to strengthen as it separates us from what we seek; that distances us from our desires, dreams and destiny? How do we satisfy this space? What do we occupy it with? What do we throw away? Why must we remain a candidate and never a captain, always auditioning but never acting? Why am I always stuck? Sometimes this space screams, sometimes it sings and sometimes it just simmers in silence. What is that silence? What is that sound? What is that smell? What is this that I now see? Why am I seeing this and not something else? So what is my next step?

We write by writing, cook by cooking, dance by dancing and take steps by stepping. The gap garners strength only when we stop stepping and sink into a hopeless, helpless and confused state. But this gap becomes a gift when we suddenly observe new but obvious opportunities; realizing that at the climax of every crisis, conflict, collapse or change lays a catalyst for courage and creativity. Everything happens for a reason but now you have awakened to the artistry and abundance of these reasons and can respond to them, reinvent them. As you receive and rejoice in these reasons, another gap will soon grow as a signal, another sign for you to renew your reasons and keep stepping. Nothing is static. We only drown if we stop swimming. Steps that are safe and secure will not suffice; each step is a romance with the unfamiliar, untamed and untested. Something new awaits, something alive. Do not settle for the same stuff merely for the sake of security. Keep stepping until you evolve into the understanding that there was never a gap in the first place.

No one saves us but ourselves. No one can and no one may.
We ourselves must walk the path.

- Buddha

Sink into each step.
Savor it,
Don't float
And be absolutely fascinated
With all the fumbling
That frequently
And ferociously forbids
The flourishing of our flesh.
They serve as the fuel to freedom.

But refrain from furthering
Your fumblings
And failures
By freezing
In the face of your fears,
Frustrations,
Or fatigue.

If you know the Way, then you know the goal, because the goal is not at the very end of the Way, the goal is all along the Way –
each moment and each step it is there.

- Osho

Move,
And keep moving
With the mysteries,
And miracles
Of each moment.

Walk,
And keep walking
As you welcome
The whispers and wisdom
Of the Way.

The Tao is referred to as the "Way" or "The Pathless Path."
The Way is unpaved and unpredictable, therefore, one cannot
rely on readymade routines and rituals; one must walk the
Way and find out for themselves. Lao Tzu was the first to
glorify the Way, or the journey and not the goal, not the end
result. The Way is alive, contributing, growing, changing,
pulsating and permeates all. Lao Tzu taught that the *Tao*
empowers the individual, not society, not the crowds and
fosters freedom, not conformity. As Osho describes it, "The
Way is not like a superhighway; the Way is like a bird flying
in the sky – it leaves no footprints behind." No two birds take
flight on the same path. It leaves no tracks but unquestionably
reaches their destination. Take your steps as a bird takes flight
– in the moment, integrated and free; soaring with sincerity,
simplicity and spontaneity.

The expert traveler
Leaves no footprints.

- Tao Te Ching

Zen Buddhism teaches that after one walks the Way, it
expands for others to enter, it does not narrow but rather
nourishes for others to enter and experience.

Roger Bannister, the British runner, who broke the 4-minute
mile in 1954, was attempting to do so in a time when this feat
was previously deemed impossible. Since then, numerous
runners and athletes from all cultures, countries and
continents have also attained this awareness of athletic artistry
to break the 4-minute mile. This is an example of expansion
and enlightenment to what is possible, within the realms of
our individual realities when we work with the Way and be
grateful for the generosity of its greatness.

*The things you do for yourself are gone when you are gone, but the
things you do for others remain as your legacy.*

- *Kalu Ndukwe Kalu, Nigerian Author*

We are fixated on our footprints.
Making a mark,
Leaving a legacy
And imposing an impression of ourselves
For others to yearn
And learn about.
Big steps,
Big,
Brave and bold,
But often belittling the boundless
Supremacy
Of small steps.

Enjoy the little things in life, for someday you will realize they were the big things.

- Robert Brault, Writer

Sweat the small stuff! Small is not reflective of size or scale but rather signifies the subtle, simple, sincere, spontaneous and sexy.

A big movement is not as effective as a small movement, a small movement is not as effective as the appearance of no movement, and it is the presence of movement within the appearance of no movement that is the real movement.

- Tai Chi Grandmaster Wang Xiang-Zhai

See simplicity in the complicated.
Achieve greatness in little things.

- Tao Te Ching

You don't set out to build a wall. You say to yourself that you are going to lay this brick as perfectly as a brick can be laid and you do that every single day.

- Will Smith, Actor

Seduced
By the speed of society,
Skipping the small,
Subtle
And simple

To sell out
And soar
Into overnight super stardom.
It takes a long time to learn how to do something simple.

- Marty Rubin, Author

In a hurry,
With nowhere to go.
Salivating to secure
The strength,
Stamina
And seduction
To satisfy the status-quo,
But simultaneously
Struggling with a spiritual stalemate.

There is more to life than just increasing its speed.

- Ghandi

Setback after setback, we stay stuck in the same struggles and
sacrifices to survive, settling for the same circumstances while
our soul spoils; soaking in self-pity and sabotage. Do not
shamefully shortchange or substitute the skillful sincerity of
our steps for superficial speed, salaries or simply for the sake
of satisfying social systems. Our steps must always serve and
share something beyond the boredom or predictability of
pretentious pursuits.

I start after my opponent begins but arrive before him.

- Tai Chi Proverb

It is not about being the tortoise or the hare,
Existence is not a race.
Remain rooted
To receive the nourishments
Of our original nature;
Relax into the rhythms
That enriches our realities.
No need to run,
No need to rush.

Often referred to, as the Yin and Yang in Buddhist meditation,
"stopping and seeing," or cessation and contemplation, is the

art of stopping delusion and seeing truth. "Stopping" or "slowing down" is not an indication of speed, timing or tempo but rather, the quality of sensitivity. The seduction of speed in our society, has destructively desensitized our abilities and awareness to savor the significance of each single step, feeling experience, moment or meal. We are in the era of expediency; short attention spans and instant gratification. Engagement in our everyday experiences is merely an exercise in brevity, not beauty. A street performer was once overheard asking his young apprentice, "Why are you rushing when you sing?! The song ain't going nowhere!"

Heaven unfolds from a single stroke.

- Chinese Proverb

We desire much,
But glory,
Greatness
And grace
Are gained through One.

I do not fear the man who has practiced ten thousand kicks once.
I fear the man who has practiced one kick ten thousand times.

- Bruce Lee

The Tao expresses the essence of One. The Original Oneness that harmonized and permeated all things. The One signifies a culmination of complete consciousness and emptiness; an all-encompassing presence that promises potential and purity in every breath and beat of the Universe. As the *Tao Te Ching* states, "The Tao gives birth to one, one gives birth to two, two gives birth to three, and three gives birth to ten thousand things." The One is beautifully summed up in the proverb, "Heaven unfolds with one stroke" or with the proverb from the Wing Chun style of martial arts, "The staff only makes one noise," The One illustrates the totality of your sincerity, technique, understanding and harmony with the Way. It reveals your romance with your craft – your intent, emotions, energy. Your sensitivity to One reflects your understanding of the whole; the completeness and significance of a single cell, song, painting, opportunity, idea or lover. As Lao Tzu famously states, " A thousand mile journey begins with a single step.

One moment of clarity, totality, spontaneity, and you burn like a flame. Just one moment is enough. One moment will make you eternal.

- Osho

Bachata Bond: The steps that we take in life, as well as dance, mirrors that of a writer's first draft – often honest but rough, raw and requires constant and creative nourishment – revising, re-reading and reinventing. This process eventually allows us to settle into our work, to relax into it until there is no any longer separation.

Bachata is balanced, basic and beautiful when we become sensitive to its subtlety, simplicity and spontaneity. Each step that we take with our partner is a step towards surrender; surrendering to her smell, spirit, sweetness and sensuality. Speed and self-satisfaction are no longer significant as we dissolve into the moment, the music, the dance and her desires.

The man, the art, the work--it is all one.

- Eugen Herrigel, Zen In the Art of Archery

Bow. Breathe. Baila Bachata.

EMOTIONS. Bachata is the art of entering, enduring and evolving our emotions – constantly revisiting and reinventing how we feel – why, for whom and for what?

The artist is a receptacle for emotions that come from all over the place: from the sky, from the earth, from a scrap of paper, from a passing shape, from a spider's web.

- Pablo Picasso

The extinction of emotions,
Endangered
By an emphasis
On our electronic ego
And efforts.

Our emotional experiences –
Internally and externally -
Left unattended,
Unanswered
And evaded entirely
As we escape endlessly
Through external ecstasy –
Drugged
With self-deception,
Denial
And distractions.

Tears have always been easier to shed than explain.

- Marty Rubin, Author

Emotionally enslaved
And exhausted
As we continue
To escape
And exercise our refusal
To renew,
Rejuvenate
And reinvent
Our experiences
And how we feel about them.

Through entering,
Not escaping,
Is how we become enriched

By our emotions.

I don't want to be at the mercy of my emotions. I want to use them, enjoy them and to dominate them.

- Oscar Wilde

We envision entry,
But can only envy
Those who actually enter.
From the outside –
The surface, the perimeter –
We continue to be embarrassed
And emasculated
By excessively entertaining
The superficial expectations
Of society
While remaining strangers
To ourselves.

We often endure
Our emotional experiences
Through escape.
We express our emotions
Through exhibitions
Of excess
And abuse;
Cold,
Carefree and suppressing
Our "downs" to artificially
Fabricate our "ups."

We seldom realize, for example that our most private thoughts and emotions are not actually our own. For we think in terms of languages and images which we did not invent, but which were given to us by our society.

- Alan Watts

The current climate and conditions of our society – desperate, imitative, electronic, violent - have effectively extinguished, suppressed and desensitized our emotions. Through the production of pretentious patterns of hope and superficial stimulation, our emotional responses have become robotic, rehearsed and deeply rooted in the past, anxiety and ego. We emotionally disengage and ferociously seek relief from our emotions - getting drunk, taking drugs, quitting, shopping and excessively eating or not eating at all – as opposed to entering; seeking and sinking into our center. We employ walls and barriers from our emotions; we do not dare feel what is real, but would rather evaluate our environments and ourselves through feeble fixations and false feelings of friends, family, fortune and freedom.

Genius is the ability to renew one's emotions in daily experience.

- Paul Cezanne, Artist

The emergence
Of our everyday emotions –
Complex,
Cloudy
And often crippling -
Is the engine
That elevates our very essence
Into the enlightened echelons
Of our expressions,
Energy
And experiences.

I write emotional algebra.

- Anais Nin

Emotions arise to be continuously examined, to explode, and elicit deep and intimate inquiry. They evoke errors as well as elation and enables us the energy, curiosity and intensity to experience the extremes of life through art, awareness, dance, music, relationships and love. Never hurry or hide any evidence of an emotional engagement with existence; in order to evolve, one must enter.

Unexpressed emotions will never die. They are buried alive and will come forth later in uglier ways.

- Sigmund Freud, Father of Psychoanalysis

Bachata Bond: The very root of Bachata, its original essence was an overflowing of emotions. Driven by emotional value, content and connection, Bachata was the vehicle to spill our guts, heart and soul - risking rejection and the ramifications of unraveling our rights to express our emotional reservoirs in the name of art, music, culture, freedom and love.

Effort and energy are usually plentiful and boundless when dancing Bachata, but the emotional experience remains elusive. Our emotional database is dim, lacking and limited, as well as superficial, undeveloped, untapped and untested. There is a lot of moving and mingling but we often miss the magic because our emotional references merely reflects the routines and rituals that are stained by greed, fear, jealousy and envy. We remain emotionally entrapped and never evolve.

Osho reminds us that the word "motion" is embedded into "emotion," to express that the nature of our emotions is impermanent, fleeting and constantly changing. Torment and torture is sure to follow if we trap our emotions, dwelling and dying, as they lay dormant in despair and desperation. We remain suppressed by the same and similar sensations over and over again. Bachateros are flooded with emotions. We engage, examine and express every emotional element that permeates our path; emphasizing the elegance and etiquette of our emotions in every lesson learned, lady loved or life lost.

Bow. Breathe. Baila Bachata.

FREEDOM. Bachata is the art of freedom – fluid, formless and fundamental.

Using no way as way, having no limitation as limitation.

- Bruce Lee

We are tired,
Tense,
Timid
And tormented daily
By the temptations
And temporary treasures
That we target,
Worship
And worry about.

Fixated
On financing phony fantasies,
As we foolishly
Forgo the fundamental faculties
Of our freedom.

Focused on flourishing
Through falsehood
And fallacies
Rather than flying
With the feathers of a falcon.

Most people do not really want freedom, because freedom involves responsibility, and most people are frightened of responsibility.

- Sigmund Freud, Father of Psychoanalysis

Foreign
To our own freedom,
We find fault
In all that we fear.

I'd rather die on my feet than live on my knees.

- Themistokles, Greek General, 300: Rise of an Empire

The frustrations of the flesh;
Fond of fame,
Fortune

And fashion,
But fatigued
And unable to fathom
Freedom
Through the Formless.

When I discover who I am, I'll be free.

- *Ralph Ellison, Invisible Man*

At the forefront of freedom,
We flourish flawlessly
By reinventing
Our own creative ratio
Of firmness,
Fluidity
And flexibility.

Never falling for the fabrications
Of form,
Formulas or formalities,
Refusing to remain
Buried in the rubble of rituals,
Religion
And race.

For most,
Freedom means Friday.
Enslaved,
Exploited and caught up
In the confinements
And conditioning
Of corporate culture.

Fearful,
And merely following
The flashy footsteps
Of fashion,
Fakes
And
Phonies.
Unable
To fly free
On our own,
We merely repeat

And regurgitate the recipes,
Routines
And roadmaps of others.

How did we so casually and unconsciously corner and convince ourselves into becoming the slaves, soldiers and servants of society? We are more chained, brainwashed dumbed-down and dependent than ever. We dare not say what we want, do what we want nor can we even think what we want. Most of us fantasize ferociously, on a daily basis, about ditching our day jobs, walking out and taking a risk to prosper on our own terms, take flight and flourish, only to snap out of it, go back to our desks and descend even deeper into desperation and despair; deep into a destructive divide of who we are, what we are doing, what we really want to be doing and who we pretend to be. Therefore, we remain drunk, depressed and detained in the systems, patterns and confinements of society.

Freedom through the Formless embodies a special feel, fabric and fragrance of freedom that few can fathom. We are too attached and shackled to everything – material, religion, status, sex – but as we all eventually figure out, it was all a fluke, a fad, fictitious. We fight hard, force and impose our will on our goals, on people, on our pursuits and in all that we believe in but ultimately, we fall short of sincere and enlightened fulfillment. We often just remain imprisoned and impersonal to ourselves and settle for living vicariously through role models, movie stars, athletes and archetypes – heroes, champions and stars.

Don't work towards freedom, but allow the work itself to be freedom.

- Dogen Roshi, Zen Master

Freedom is forever at our fingertips if we just open ourselves to new, alive and spontaneous opportunities. Osho reminds us that true freedom is rooted in responsibility; not the usual associations of responsibility – obligation, bills, duties – but rather, as he coins it, "response – ability." The more we can respond to a moment, a message or to music from our own intelligence, awareness and spontaneity, the more we fly on our own. We all seek freedom. We seek the freedom to do what we please, freedom from political, social and economic systems, along with intellectual, artistic and sexual freedom. But rarely do we find an individual who is internally illuminated, intimate and intense enough to respond. Osho distinguishes the key differences between a revolution, reform and rebellion. A revolution and reform are both engineered towards outward change, whereas, a rebellion is inward change. Only a rebel can foster inward change and let go of the past to fly free in the present. Renouncing, resisting or escaping everyday engagement is not necessary when you can consciously, creatively and courageously respond to each moment.

So one who is ready to accept the responsibility of being oneself with all its beauties, bitterness, its joys and agonies, can be free. Only such a person can be free.

- Osho

The fundamental faculty
Of our freedom –
The ability to flourish
In the face of tyranny
And any psychological,
Social
Or economical takeovers,
Is through fire.

Be a light unto yourself.

- Buddha

Fire is not a fabrication of force,
Fortitude
Or fierceness.
Fire is a fascination
With the fulfillment
Of our families,
Fortunes,
Fortresses and fitness.
Furthering the flesh
Through both form
And the Formless.

Most are too fearful,
Fragmented
And feeble

To foster their own flame.
We forget
That we are free to forge fires,
Take flight
And burn through the barriers,
Burdens
And beliefs
That blinds and buries
Our bliss.

The *Firing Process* or the *Fire Method* in Taoist traditions, were
usually exercises, meditations or techniques towards
transformation, transcendence and truth. Most of us run on
fumes and fear, therefore, our spirit is fragmented, feeble and
fabricated. Fire is the internal device used to dissolve all
deceptions, obstacles and layers to love, truth and artistry.

*Enough of these phrases, conceit and metaphors, I want burning,
burning, burning.*

- Rumi

The temperatures of man,
Transcended into tenacity,
Triumph
And truth.

Just as a flame
Can free the flavor,
Fragrance
And fabric of food,
Man must boil
And evaporate
Into eternal
Essence and effortless energy.

*Life is fire, it is a function of fire, without fire life cannot exist.
Without the sun there will be no trees, no men, no birds, no
animals. It is transformed fire that becomes life.*

- Osho

Like a chef,
Masters of temperatures;
Providers and poets
Of heat transfer

And transcendence.
From frozen
And cold –
Callous, impenetrable, impersonal –
To compassionate
And conscious;
Lukewarm to legendary.

Rehearse death. To say this is to tell a person to rehearse his freedom. A person who has learned how to die has unlearned how to be a slave.

- Seneca, Roman Philosopher

Bachata Bond: We all have the freedom to live and dance according to our own artistic aspirations and visions, but few do. We have the energy to explode, but yet we choose to escape Existence and evade our experiences with excuses. We willingly choose to imprison our dreams, potential and ideas for the sake of staying safe, well behaved and secure in the eyes and systems of society. The reason for this is because most of us have never felt fire in our bellies or under our butts. Reignite your internal flame; your fire to fly, and you will be free.

Bow. Breathe. Baila Bachata.

CONNECTING. Are we actually connecting with our culture or just unconsciously conforming?

Wherever you are, you are one with the clouds and one with the sun and the stars you see. You are one with everything. That is more that I can say, and more true than you can hear.

- Shunryu Suzuki, Zen Master

Our contemporary culture
Of connection
And connectivity –
Technologically heavy
And digitally dominant –
We are glued
To our gadgets
And defined by our devices.

Dig deeper
Into this digital dependence
And you will demystify
The dynamics
Of all our current deficiencies,
Dysfunctions
And disappointments.
What appears to qualify
As connection in our culture
Is merely a curriculum
For control.

Whenever you find yourself on the side of the majority, it's time to pause and reflect.

- Mark Twain, American Author

The current climate
Of connectivity
In our culture
Has cultivated crowds
Of unconscious
And compulsive consumers;
Carelessly craving
And "clicking"
Their way into the corridors
Of conflict,

Complexity
And conformity.

I think the reward for conformity is that everyone likes you except yourself.

- Rita Mae Brown, American Author

We conform
To the destructiveness
Of common conduct
Concerns and convictions –
Comparing,
Competing
And always caught up
In the commotion
Of catching the next consumer craze.

Accumulating confidence
And comfort
Through cars,
Clothes
And cash,
While resting
On the conveniences
Of our lies,
Masks
And limitations.

We are currently strengthening a crisis in contemporary
communication and connectivity. What may appear to be
connection and conveniences in our daily doings are actually
all just illusions of connection. We are more cold, isolated,
impersonal, imitative and inconsiderate than ever. We occupy
ourselves with the same gossip, confrontations, television
shows and trends as everyone else. We all shop at the same
stores, wear the same clothes, use the same devices and
computers, rely on the same services, bank with the same
banks; the full spectrum of human conscience, conduct,
capabilities and cravings have been controlled, conditioned
and digitally dictated, tracked and analyzed. We are captured
by categorization, classified by class and controlled as
cowards. Cowards operate in crowds and are weak, divided,
defiant and destructive; coerced to participate in crime,

catastrophe and corruption. We are all "connected" only from a position of dependence, fear, greed, envy and lies.

We cannot solve our problems with the same thinking we used when we created them.

- *Albert Einstein*

Consciousness
Is the only criterion
For connection.
It also serves as the key
To cracking the code
Of contemporary control
And conditioning;
Killing
The common culprits
That clouds,
Contaminates
And conceals our consciousness.

We correct
And cleanse
By being congruent,
And calibrated
With our consciousness;
Choosing clarity,
Creativity
And courage
Over commotion
And compulsion.

A lot of people in our industry haven't had very diverse experiences. So they don't have enough dots to connect, and they end up with very linear solutions without a broad perspective on the problem. The broader one's understanding of the human experience, the better design we will have.

- Steve Jobs, Founder of Apple Computers

The Buddha taught us that the root cause of all suffering was our constant craving, clinging and desiring. This desiring has dragged us into deep discontent and has magnified our daily difficulties. We are divided, disconnected and disingenuous towards our own voice, visions and values. The more we accumulate, the more attached, dependent and imprisoned we will be come. Free of clinging and complexities, however, we become formless, fluid, flexible and free.

From the very beginning, all beings are buddhas.

- Hakuin Ekaku, Zen Buddhist

We were born
And blessed as Buddhas
But we started to accumulate;
Allowing things,
Thoughts,
Theories
And the cunning theatrics
Of a seductive society
To take up space.

Material possession you hold to be valuable are your enemies.
Come with nothing when you shoot.

- Master Awa Kenzo, Zen in the Art of Archery

Dissolve
Into the depths
And details
Of your daily defeats,
Disappointments
And delays.
Dare to detach
From the detrimental devices,
Deeds and dialogues
That depletes
And destroys your dimples.

Darkness gives light a place to shine.

- Lao Tzu

Consciousness
Is our light
To love,
Laugh
And live.

Bachata Bond: We are all seeking more meaning and deeper connections in our everyday lives – spiritually, artistically, romantically or sexually. We aim to be more aligned, aware and closer to all that we desire, envision and love. But all our efforts, tips, tricks and rituals to achieve this connection, this congruence, synchronicity and satisfaction are often elusive and deflate us into hopelessness and confusion.

The clarity and depth of all our connections are directly related to the quality of our consciousness. We cannot connect if we are not conscious; we could go through the motions, wish or spectate from the surface or the perimeter but we would not be connected. We could be reading a book, but be totally disengaged and occupied by a million other thoughts and worries; completely disconnected so we wind up reading the same page over and over again. Everything is, was and will always be connected – people, places, events, energies, thoughts. But we compromise this connection by conforming and converting into the classes, categories and common conclusions of our culture. We are not obligated to robotically pursue the priorities, pressures and promotions of society or to mold ourselves after the modern motives and mentality of the masses. Commit to creatively and courageously connecting with your craft, relationships and everyday existence by awakening to your consciousness.

In our weird and wired world, the art of Bachata still has the capacity to cultivate consciousness and bring beauty back to the natural bond we have with our bodies. Bachata begins with a connection of bodies, which elevates into expressions of eternity. This is only possible through the quality of your consciousness. Consciousness gives you a glimpse into your greatness, your gifts, your Godliness. Our connection to our partner, the music, lyrics, culture and to the moment is the core of this dance, this art. We are still connected to and touched by people that we danced with hours, days, months or even years ago. Be present, intimate, engaged and meditative – this is to be conscious.

Unplug and dance.

Bow. Breathe. Baila Bachata.

WAR. It is a war out there. *We* have turned it into a war.
Bring it back to a dance.

Weak mind, weak fist; strong mind no need for fist.

- *Shaolin Kung Fu Proverb*

The will to win in this world
Has warranted a withdrawal
From our wealth,
Wisdom
And wings
From within.

We have instead welcomed
The workmanship of
Brutes,
Brawlers and bankers
To battle
And beckon bloodshed
By waging warfare -
Informational, psychological, emotional,
Social, economical, political –
On our whims,
Worries
And all the worthless
Things we worship.

I practice the art of fighting without fighting.

- *Bruce Lee*

Only the weak
Wavers to the whims of
Man-made warfare,
Allowing the world
To taint the treasures
That were already
Deeply woven
Into the whispers
Of within.

Jabbing and jousting
Between joy,
Justice

And jealousy,
Worrying about the war
That never was.

Osho uses the term "jungle" as an analogy to describe the darkness and deep sleep that the modern man marinates in; stumbling, groping and full of desires but aimless and at the mercy of every whim. The jungle mentality begs, bargains and latches on to every superstition, fad or gimmick. They continue to perform the routines and rituals of recycled religions; respected and approved by society but heavily controls and separates the hearts of humanity through fear, guilt and worship for the sake of reward and punishment. Refrain from all religious warfare and sew the seeds to sincere spirituality; honing Heaven on Earth, not through the hoopla of hate and havoc. The Higher is hidden in the hints, hues, humor and happiness of our own homes, hearts and hands; peace and power in plain sight. Secure the seduction of our stars, seas and soil, capture the communication from the qualities of our clouds and climate, talk with our trees and merge into the magnificence of our mountains. Spirituality is just that; a sincere and spontaneous awareness to the extraordinary of the Ordinary; the elegance of everyday. No need to seek secrets, powers and authority in sacred books, men in costumes or brainwashing behaviors, beliefs and rituals.

Religion has convinced people that there's an invisible man living in the sky. Who watches everything you do every minute of every day. And the invisible man has a list of ten specific things he doesn't want you to do. And if you do any of these things, he will send you to a special place, of burning and fire and smoke and torture and anguish for you to live forever, and suffer, and suffer, and burn, and scream, until the end of time. But he loves you. He loves you. He loves you and he needs money.

- George Carlin, Comedian

Withdraw from the war that never was;
Embellishing enemies
And exaggerations
That never existed.
Unload all burdens –
Envy, ego, excess –

To bring bliss
And beauty back to our bodies.
Become weightless,
Not allowing worthless worries
And woes to weaken
And weigh us down.

Stop wrestling with your right
To receive –
Working, whining,
Waiting,
And wishing
While witnessing
The destruction
Of your dreams,
Desires
And dignity.

I do not try to dance better than anyone else. I only try to dance better than myself.

- Mikhail Baryshnikov, Dancer

Win from within,
Witness yourself as the
Window
To worldly influence,
Innovation
And integration.

Walk away from wages
To welcome wealth,
Waste not another wish,
And march right through
All the imaginary walls –
Psychological, emotional, spiritual, sexual –
Of worldly warfare.

Stealing,
Stabbing, struggling
And salivating over symbols
And status
While the welfare,
Warmth and wishes
Of our women

Are wounded
And go to waste.

We are constantly seeking outward change – economical,
social, religious and political. Restless and relentless for
reform but refusing responsibility to reinvent our responses to
the very things that we find repulsive; only repeating the
routines that ruin us. We argue, fight and hate the
establishment and all the empires of evil but warfare is
worthless and only further deepens our desperation,
deterioration and division within ourselves. Without war, we
win by working with the Way and the wisdom of weather,
wildlife, water, Wing Chun and our women. You *are* the
expression, energy and establishment that you envision.

Be the change that you wish to see in the world.

- Mahatma Gandhi

Bachata Bond: This is the first and foremost form of warfare - a
fierce but futile fight within ourselves. We withhold our
wisdom, will and worth; wrapped up, tangled and tormented
in worldly and internal warfare, wobbling through life as a
representative; a robotic rendition of society's servants and
soldiers. We operate and introduce ourselves only as a
representative; some twisted perception of who we think we
should be and how we should behave, constantly revising,
repeating and reassuring our act according to the approval of
crowds, cowards and corporate carbon copies. Withdraw
from this war, as there is no enemy, no evil and no
establishment that can ever enter if one embodies the energy,
etiquette and enlightenment of the Eastern Engine.

We often meet ourselves too late in life. Spending years and
years participating, reacting and revolving our peace, potential
and priorities around the rhythms and roles of the rat race. We
continue battling with brain-dead brutes and barbarians while
welcoming worthless wars around worldly gains and glamour;
only to block the paths to our own voice, vision and vastness.

The warfare of Bachata – condemning, criticizing and
comparing schools, styles, teachers, techniques and tradition.
Students, teachers and watchers remain reckless within;
dividing oneself through thoughts and feelings of being

inadequate, inferior and incapable of performing at certain levels, while others believe the opposite and remain insistent on imposing their superiority, stuck on skill and sequence but never satisfying the spontaneous quality of the dance. While the weak continue to whine, worry and waste every waking moment to war, our women wait for worthy warriors to welcome them to the Way, and dance into the dreams of their deepest, darkest and most decadent desires.

Stop worrying about the work, wishes and will of others, And start worshipping the wonder, wisdom and wings that we house from within. Osho reminds us that heaven and hell have nothing to do with geography. Heaven is our awareness, a conscious state of creativity, whereas, hell is exactly where we are, unconscious, asleep and held captive to all the confinements and conditionings of society.

Bow. Breathe. Baila Bachata.

FEELING. Bachata is the art of feeling.

It is not enough to know your craft – you have to have feeling.
Science is all very well, but for us imagination is worth far more.

- Edouard Manet, Artist

Gut feelings,
Good feelings,
Bad feelings,
Funny and fuzzy feelings;
How do we feel
What we feel?
And how do we not feel
What we do not feel?

Whether through tears,
Talking
Or touch,
We crave
And cling to
Familiar feelings.

Feelings that fosters
Our happiness,
Health,
Relationships
And successes;
While also remaining fixated
On the feelings that fatigue
And fluster us.

The best and most beautiful things in the world cannot be seen
or even touched. They must be felt with the heart.

- Helen Keller

We are obsessed with our feelings. We exercise, work, invest,
play, perform, date and diet to feel good about ourselves; to
feel proud, generous, ambitious and accomplished. But why is
it that more often than not, our efforts to foster intentional
feelings leave us frustrated, fearful and unfulfilled? Fabricating
feelings for the sake of familiarity is safe but not spontaneous.
We must also get a feeling for all that is foreign and formless.

185

The best goose bumps, chills and butterflies come from the mysterious, the unexpected and the unknown.

Some people feel the rain. Others just get wet.

- Bob Marley

The confusion of contact –
Physical, visual, verbal, emotional, spiritual –
We touch
And become touched,
By teachers,
Technology, techniques, truth
And tears
But all forms of contact
Continues to be cold,
Careless,
Controlling
And condemning.

Anybody can learn to think, or believe, or know, but not a single human being can be taught to feel... the moment you feel, you're nobody-but-yourself - in a world which is doing its best, night and day, to make you everybody else - means to fight the hardest battle which any human being can fight, and never stop fighting.

- E.E. Cummings

Our tactile temptations –
Tapping,
Typing and toying
With machines
And devices all day;
Our touch is tamed,
Tasteless,
Desensitized
And no longer a tool
To transform and transcend.

Touch comes before sight, before speech. It is the first language and the last, and it always tells the truth.

- Margaret Atwood, Writer

Hands and fingertips function as our catalyst for contact, connection, creativity, comfort and compassion in dance.

They are the entry points and receptacles to receive messages as well as our extensions to express energy, etiquette, curiosity and interest. *Mudras* (moo-druhs) are Buddhist hand gestures and positions that promote health, clarity, energy flow, peace and receptivity. There are numerous combinations of different gestures and positions. Just like letters are used in a variety of ways to form different words, each finger is touching, twisting and bending to create different feelings, blessings, effects and messages. A very common mudra is the *Gyan* mudra, where the tip of the index finger touches the tip of the thumb while the palm is facing up and the other three fingers are extended out and together. This gesture stimulates wisdom, calmness and compassion. When you are dancing with your partner, you are performing mudras; simultaneously sending and receiving a multitude of messages that mirrors your feelings, enthusiasm, intent and intensity. The fornication of fingers facilitates the foreplay that, ultimately, finds and fulfills fantasies far and beyond the flesh.

Touch has memory.

- John Keats, English Poet

A dancer feels.
They do not deliberate
The delicacies of
Timing and rhythm
Through theories,
Techniques,
Terminology
Or technology.

Dance first. Think later. That is the natural order.

- Samuel Becket, Irish Novelist

A dancer
Interprets
The intervals of space,
Sound
And sequence
Through the internal instruments
Of intimacy,
Intensity,
Intuition and instincts.

187

Don't think – FEEL.

- Bruce Lee, Martial Artist, Founder of Jeet Kuen Do

The Japanese term *Maai* translates to "distance" and is often used to describe the moving and changing qualities of near and far. Ancient Japanese warriors believed that Maai was the most important aspect of combat and swordsmanship and was usually coupled with the concept of *Hyoshi*, the term that references the relation, balance and harmony of cadence and rhythm. Everything in combat embodies cadence and rhythm, from the swing of your sword to the beat of your heart. *Yomi* is the Japanese concept that literally translates to "reading" and is often described as "the art of sensing and foreseeing the moves or movements of the adversary." Master swordsman and legend, Miyamoto Musashi, author of the *Book of Five Rings*, disregarded tactics, texts and techniques when it came to combat to prevent conditioned responses, anxious anticipation or premature maneuvers. He relied rather, on sensitivity, feeling and experience.

I've learned that people will forget what you said, people will forget what you did, but people will never forget how you made them feel.

- Maya Angelou

Thinking
And trying in combat,
As in dancing,
Is merely useful for practice
And controlled circumstances
But utterly useless
When applied to anything
That is alive,
Awake
And authentic – an adversary,
Partner,
Music or to a moment.

The world's pulse is our pulse.
The world's rhythms are our rhythms.

- Tao Te Ching

188

Timing and rhythm are perhaps two of the most significant and subtle sources to how we engage our environment, relationships, businesses and ideas. But what exactly is timing? My time is not your time and your time is not my time. So what is the right time and who or where has that time? As Alan Watts describes it, "Time is merely a mechanism to measure, to communicate and convene, or how else would we meet? How would you know when and where to meet me?" We are taught right from the beginning to tell time, manage time, balance time, save time and never waste time but, ultimately, we become trapped in the templates, terminology and technological tautologies of time. Most of us interpret and associate time with numeric representations through clocks, calendars and computers. But is that what time is? And must the rhythms of our lives be ruled by the standards, structures and systems that have been conveniently preset by society?

Life, if thou know how to use it, is long enough.

- Seneca, Philosopher

Dominated by the digital rhythms
And technologies of society,
We must recapture
And rekindle our rapport
And romance
With the rhythms of rocks,
Rivers
And Rain.

Everything in the universe has rhythm. Everything dances.

- Maya Angelou

As within,
So without.
This is the profound Taoist perspective
That timing and rhythm
Are both within us
And reflects out,
Therefore,
We must relax into our rhythms
And transcend timing
Into temperature,

Turning points
And truth.

Timing, like the Tao, is all around us, all-inclusive and
permeates us. Time is abundant, available and accessible if
we just awaken to it. Remove the destructive, violent and
ritualized rhythms of society. There is no need to ever rush,
race, resist or overreach for anything that you were naturally
rightful to receive. Synchronize with your whispers within. To
transcend time past the confinements, concepts and control of
clocks and calendars is to tune in to the tutelage of
timelessness. The only time that exists is the eternity we
experience in the present moment, the herenow.

Never is impatient,
But all is done on time.

- Tao Te Ching

*You have to keep your reflexes so that when you want it — it's
there. When you want to move — you are moving. And when you
move, you are determined to move! Not accepting even one inch
less than 100 percent of your honest feelings. Not anything less
than that. So that is the type of thing you have to train yourself
into. To become one with your feelings so that, when you think —
it is.*

- Bruce Lee

Bachata Bond: Our feelings form and flourish through the
Formless. Yoga, cars, clothes and cash can fabricate familiar
feelings and states of "feel good" but are all usually fleeting
and fictitious. These fabricated feelings are usually just the
manifestations of mass marketing and artificial accumulation.

Feelings that simmer and grow within the thresholds of the
Formless are that which facilitates the freedom to internal
timing and rhythms. We must develop and savor our
sensitivity to the sounds, sights and space from within, in
relation to the world without; therefore, we will never
flustered or fatigued by the noises, expectations and standards
of our society. This is when we find ourselves at the right
place at the right time; randomly finding a twenty-dollar bill,

meeting a lover, catching a train or landing a life-changing opportunity.

Feeling, timing and rhythm are all integral and internal aspects of Bachata. We begin to know where things are without actually looking, we move without any manipulation of external influences or insecurities and we continue to touch without actually physically touching. It was an internal flame, a fire that originally facilitated the foundations of Bachata. That flame still touches us today through culture, movement, music, spirit and celebrations. As Bachateros, we must always continue to renew and rejuvenate our feelings, timing and rhythms; never settling for the same stale sensations.

Bow. Breath. Baila Bachata.

THE UNKNOWN. Unravel the unknown by unlearning, unlistening and unlocking all the limitations that have lead to losing and lacking; leaving us lingering in lies, lust and loneliness.

Man can learn nothing except by moving from the known to the unknown.

- Claude Bernard, Writer

The unawakened man,
Unequipped,
Uncommitted
And unwilling
To untie
The knots of the unnecessary
Or burn the baggage
That bottles up
Their best.

One is never afraid of the unknown; one is afraid of the known coming to an end.

- Jiddu Krishnamurti

Refusing to release
The restrictions
Rules,
And rituals
Of our ridiculous renderings of "reality;"
Thus unable
To make room
For the triumphs
And treasures
Of the unrealistic,
Uncommon
And the unknown.

How can you know what you're capable of if you don't embrace the unknown?"

- Esmeralda Santiago, Puerto Rican Author

We continue to downplay and dismiss the rewards of navigating new roads and reinventing our realities to abandon the predictable, the average. Most are unwilling to undertake

the torrents and turbulences of uncharted waters and thereby
must settle for the true, tried and tested. We remain timid and
deterred by the untamed, terrified by the tenacity of what we
cannot easily take.

I wasted time, and now doth time waste me.

- *William Shakespeare*

The roadblocks of our reality, repeatedly remind us to resist
any risks to renew and rejuvenate the old; fearing failure and a
blemished reputation. We are persuaded by past precedents,
performances and public perceptions; thus, we persist in
personal poverty and, ultimately, postponement to the
possibilities of recruiting new relationships, rewards and
romances.

*Two thirds of the earth's surface is ocean, and all we can see of it
with the naked eye is the surface: the skin. We hardly know
anything about what's beneath the skin.*

- *Haruki Murakami, The Wind-Up Bird Chronicle*

Unveil the unknown,
Invite
The unintended,
Embrace
The unexpected
And welcome the worse.

Not until we are lost do we begin to find ourselves.

- *Henry David Thoreau, American Author and Poet*

Uncover
Every corner
Of existence
With unconditional,
Uncontaminated and uncompromising
Creativity and courage
Along with an unflinching
Level of love,
Despite your upbringing,
Employment
Or education.

To attain knowledge, add things every day; to attain wisdom, subtract things every day.

- Lao Tzu

Most of us are uncomfortable with the unknown. We are uncertain and unarmed to understand what is uncommon, unorthodox or unpredictable, therefore we remain utterly useless and unable to receive or respond to anything new. Michelangelo, master artist, once said that there is no idea, no possibility and no concept that is not contained within a single piece of marble once you start to eliminate the excess; that the main job of an artist was to free the angel that waits patiently within. Strip off the fat that forbids your freedom, fortune and fragrance from unfolding and free the angel within yourself that patiently awaits your awakening.

Art is the elimination of the unnecessary.

- Pablo Picasso. Artist

Keep filling your bowl,
and it will spill over.

Keep sharpening your knife,
And it will blunt.

Keep hoarding gold in your house,
And you will get robbed.

- Tao Te Ching

Unburden yourself
From the bridges that burn you,
Unchain yourself
From the choices that trap you,
Let it all go
And allow light
To illuminate
Your love.

Demote the darkness
That had once deceived you
And capture a creative,
Cultural

And cosmic comprehension
Of the unspoken,
Unwritten
And unseen.
Uplift
And unleash your love
And courage
In the unadulterated underbelly
Of the unknown.

Simplicity is the ultimate form of sophistication.

- Leonardo da Vinci

Talk less,
Leave your limitations
By letting go of laziness
And your lust
For luxury.

The less I needed, the better I felt.

- Charles Bukowski, German American Poet

Unload all logic
That latches on to hate,
Jealously
And fruitless fear.
Be absolutely uncomfortable
With all the comforts,
Conveniences
And consistencies
Of a conditioned society.
Disconnect
From its captivity
And remain unaffected
By the unnecessary
And unnatural.

The greatest carver does the least cutting.

- Lao Tzu

We pride ourselves on the paths, passions and products that
we pursue; praying that it will all propel our potential to
permanent power and prosperity. But why is it that our

195

pursuits often only push us to the pinnacle of pain, plateaus and poverty? We live in a world where passionate painters are waiting tables; whining, worrying and worthlessly wishing to paint for a living. Where musicians, actors and actresses aspire to awaken, stir and stun the soul, spirit and psyche of the masses, but often just silently submit to their struggles and settle for side jobs. We panic and become personally pressured, perplexed and petrified of the unpredictable. It is urgent that we drop all preconceived practices, perversions and preferences to unveil an unblemished, unprecedented and unpaved path. This will undoubtedly transcend your travels into the unknown; making your dreams, desires and deeds undeniable and your success unstoppable. As Master Sun Tzu teaches in the *Art of War*, "The best opportunities come from the unexpected."

Bachata Bond: The early beginnings of Bachata encountered and endured extreme economical, political and social resistance. Bachata was considered to be artistically, aesthetically and academically inferior to the existing popular genres of salsa and merengue. Equipped with only the essentials of energy and emotion, our Bachateros endured and broke through brutal barriers by bonding in bars, backyards and beaches. Unaccepted but undeterred; from underground and underdog to unifying and uplifting a country with lyrics, laughter, love and an unwillingness to waver even an inch on the worth and will of their music, art and feelings.

Bachateros embrace the unknown; unfazed by the unfamiliar, we are prepared to enter untapped territory to fight for what fuels our freedom. With Bachata, every opportunity, every moment in the dance should be a deep and daring adventure into the unknown, and perhaps even the unknowable; remaining mysterious and magical. Everything should be new. The unknown is always communicating with us, inviting us, welcoming us; always in motion, always communicating, changing, and challenging us. Bring our women into the unknown; forgo all our fruitless and feeble fetishes and unfold the feasts and fantasies that awaits us.

Do not imprison and immobilize this dance through the confinements of concepts, control, techniques and routines. Be unpredictable and savor spontaneity. Bachata, as well as life, is too precious to persist in the predictable, the known.

Eliminate your emphasis on excess and unburden yourself from past baggage and beliefs. We are accustomed and conditioned to accumulate more and more but entering the unknown requires us to unload the unnecessary. Enter with emptiness and remain completely open, attentive and appreciative to all that is available to you. There is no dabbling or any halfway attempts in the unknown, it's all in, all the way, all the time. Often times in the unknown and unknowable realms of our Existence, either expressed though adversity, evil or change; theories, advice and conventional wisdom will not do. We just have to clamp down and rely on the power and purity of pure presence. Call it what you please – guts, will, god – but there will be moments when it will be just you and the air that you have left to breathe.

Do not be distracted by insignificant movements of the sword.

- Miyomoto Musashi

Bow. Breathe. Baila Bachata.

EFFORTLESS. We are entertaining an era where everyone envisions an epic entrance into economic excess; endlessly elaborating our electronic ego and efforts to entice the eyeballs of our enemies, entities and the envious.

Boards don't hit back.

- Bruce Lee, Enter the Dragon

The ethics and ethos of our efforts –
Empowered by ego,
Excess
And expediency;
Emphasized
Through external exhibitions.

Striving endlessly
To be exciting,
Exceptional
And enchanting to everyone
And everything
Except for ourselves.

The less effort, the faster and more powerful you will be.

- Bruce Lee

In the classic film, "Enter the Dragon," Bruce Lee's adversary breaks a board with a hand strike right in his face before battle, as means for intimidation. Bruce Lee famously responded by stating, "Boards don't hit back." Breaking the board served mostly as an exhibition – solely to satisfy one's ego. Most of us are just "breaking boards." We are completely ecstatic and enamored over our efforts, feeling good about ourselves, convincing others of our happiness, staying busy, active and endlessly entertaining our ego. We strive to justify the significance of our existence by establishing worldly objectives and obsessions, while employing exotic expectations as executives of our own estates and empires. But these efforts only ever ensure emotional emptiness and repeated intervals of insecurity; always incomplete and wanting more. Nothing you gain is actually what you were striving for. When we cease to find joy, satisfaction and fulfillment in shiny metals, plastics and leather, we begin to enter the essence of effortless doing, being and living.

Effortless energy and action, or as Lao Tzu describes it, "action without interference," is a natural state of engagement; numb to narcissism and the need to be artificially known, accepted, admired or applauded.

Only that which is attained through effortlessness will never be a burden to you.

- Osho

We emulate excellence
By endlessly salivating
Towards the typical –
Temporary treasures,
Titles
And trophies.

Firm,
Focused
And fixated on flourishing
As we fight
To finance our phony fantasies
To fame,
Fashion
And fortune.
Faces fatigued,
Fake
And ultimately fooled
By fictitious flattery.

Life etches itself onto our faces as we grow older, showing our violence excesses or kindnesses.

- Rembrandt, Dutch Painter

The *Tao*, or the Way, was used by Lao Tzu to describe "the natural course" of things. Lao Tzu taught the notion of "non-action," that is, acting without interfering, loving without possessing and accomplishing great things without claiming credit. This is the essence of effortlessness, the true embodiment of the Eastern Engine. To be effortless in everyday experiences, encounters and endeavors is to elevate towards the essential, not the superficial. This means that we are effortlessly easing into existence by enjoying and expanding our energy and expressions through intimacy, intensity and integration; exemplifying excellence by eliminating our enemies – envy, excess and ego.

The Way of Heaven
Is to be skilled at winning without striving.

- Tao Te Ching

We extinguish our efforts
By striving,
Struggling
And sacrificing aimlessly
And aggressively.
Arrogantly engineering everything –
Social,
Political, ecological, agricultural
And genetic engineering –
Exchanging the essential
For the artificial,
Chemicals
Contaminating everything
From ketchup to consciousness.
This is the eventual extinction
Of our emotional
And environmental empowerment.

What we are doing to the forests of the world is but a mirror reflection of what we are doing to ourselves and to one another.

- Mahatma Gandhi, Indian Civil Rights Activist

Without excessive
Force
Or fabrication,
The eloquence
Of effortless energy
Echoes the wisdom
And wonder of water.

Empty your mind, be formless. Shapeless like water. If you put water into a cup, it becomes the cup. You put water into a bottle and it becomes the bottle. You put it in a teapot, it becomes the teapot. Now, water can flow or it can crash. Be water, my friend.

- Bruce Lee

Lao Tzu wisely observed that the soft, supple and yielding, like a newborn baby, plants and flowers, are companions of life, while the hard, brittle and dry are of death. The mightiest tree is the first to crack in a storm while the grass simply absorbs its energy. Lao Tzu emphasized fluidity, flexibility and freedom. He further states, "The supreme good is like water, which nourishes all things without trying to." Long labor, working hard, blood, sweat and tears is what we glorify, what we admire and teach, but the education, eloquence and energy of water is the complete opposite.

> Nothing under heaven is more yielding than water;
> But when it attacks things hard and resistant,
> There is not one of them that can prevail.
> That the yielding conquers the resistant
> And the soft conquers the hard
> Is a fact known by all men,
> But utilized by none.

- Tao Te Ching

Water is the driving force of nature.

- Leonardo da Vinci

With the will of the Way
And the wisdom
Of water within us,
We evolve
And enter
The elevated echelons of energy,
The etiquette of emptiness.

> We shape clay
> To birth a vessel,
> Yet it's the hollow within
> That makes it useful.

- Tao Te Ching

As Lao Tzu says, "The usefulness of the cup is in its emptiness." As in art, the negative space is just as important as the positive, they are complementary and therefore one cannot exist without the other; there can be no front without a back and no back without a front. Emptiness does not exclude, it is all encompassing, like space housing our stars and planets, infinite and inexhaustible. Emptiness is the elimination of ego and all clinging, conditioning and limitations. When you embody the essence of emptiness, no longer enclosed, existence emphatically and unconditionally unleashes its love, loyalty and luxuries to you. Osho reminds us that when we purchase a house, we purchase the visible – the walls, the material, the aesthetics. But can you live in the material? Can you live in the walls? You have to live in the room, in the vacant space." That is the emphasis. In the emptiness is where you grow family, welcome guests and celebrate. Emptiness is enjoying existence.

Suckered
Into solidifying just the surface,
Skin deep,
Servant to the superficial,
Sacrificing
For the perishable,
And predictable.

The poorer we are inwardly, the more we try to enrich ourselves outwardly.

- Bruce Lee

We are empowered by economical endeavors and pursuits, but remain burdened by loss. Everything that we have worked so hard to achieve, accumulate and aggressively acquire can easily be taken away, controlled, contaminated or attacked – status, jewels, reputation – either emotionally, physically or psychologically. But the essence and elegance of emptiness embodies eternal energy and cannot be exploited, exhausted, possessed or stolen. We seek to be efficient, productive, competent and valuable but as Chuang Tzu reminds us, when we seek to be somebody, we suffer. We are not present; we are not alert, not aware, not responding, only planning, projecting and pursuing a personality that we hope will propel us to prosperity. We continue to gather and tightly grip our goods for a glimpse of glamour, gain and glory; not realizing that we are only deepening our descent into dissatisfaction.

One tree makes a million match sticks, but only one matchstick is needed to burn a million trees.

- Unknown

Bachata Bond: Effortless does not equate to easy. Effortless energy and etiquette embodies trusting, knowing, believing, relaxing and relating. There is never a need to force or overreach aimlessly and arrogantly. The elevated echelons of energy and excellence are exposed in the everyday expressions of our extraordinary earth. Through effortlessness, we ease into the elegance of Existence.

This is the essence and foundation of the classic Chinese internal martial art styles of Tai Chi, Xing-Yi and Bua Gua. Masters of these arts teaches one to welcome the energy and will of an opponent, not colliding or clashing with it. The power of softness and subtlety are the sources of their supremacy. This is usually the complete opposite of what we are encouraged to emphasize in the marketplace. We are pushed to be useful, productive, powerful and precise – obsessed with being occupied and always eager to exhibit our efforts. Unfortunately, this approach usually leaves most of us exhausted, enraged, exploited and embarrassed.

Chuang Tzu teaches us to understand the usefulness in the "useless." Smiling is useless, hugging is useless, enjoying a breeze is useless, listening to raindrops is useless, looking deep into the eyes of your loved ones is useless, smelling a flower is useless, laughing with children is useless and observing the moon and mountains are useless. But it is usually during these moments, when we engage with the "useless," that we are most alive, aware and artistic. We enjoy the effortlessness of these experiences and are enriched by them.

The Universe will always evolve through the energy and expressions of artists, dancers and conscious creators. They are relaxed and lost in a romance few can ever imagine. They can literally die doing what they do, whether or not they are getting paid for it or if anyone is watching. Bachata emphasizes effortless energy, not just an exhibition of efforts rooted in ego. People try and practice for years and years, but the dance never becomes natural to them. They remain stiff, mechanical and rooted in their efforts, rather than letting go and allowing the dance to unfold. Effortlessness emanates from spontaneity and the potential of the present moment.

Bow. Breathe. Baila Bachata.

INTIMACY. Intimacy is the art of internal illumination. It is the interaction with the Invisible, the Infinite and the Immeasurable.

All that is impossible is impersonal,
All that is internal is inevitable.

An intensification
Of idiots
In our world
Has been interfering
With the initiatives
And innovations
Of internally illuminated individuals.

The person who says something is impossible should not
interrupt the person who is doing it.

- Chinese Proverb

Idiots are a condition, a quality, a result of men and women who have been isolated, controlled, manipulated and influenced by all institutions – religious, political, social – and serve as the sacrificial servants and slaves to society. We must ignore the indecencies and illnesses of idiots.

The insecurity of idiots,
Quick to idolize
And satisfy
All the spineless suggestions of society
Before securing the serenity
Of one's own soul
Silence
And spirit.

Immersed
In all that is imitative
And impersonal,
The idiot
Remains inadequate,
Inferior
And incomplete.

We remain manipulated by the "machine," the "matrix," the man-made markets of our modern day engine. Our interactions are digitally dominant; merging mindlessly into the mannerisms of machines and trending towards transactions that are mainly technologically driven. Therefore, we are often irritated, irrational, ignorant and insufficient as we rests our survival solely on external advancements, appraisals and answers. We are becoming dangerously and destructively incapable of internally instructing ourselves; we are internally illiterate.

I was not designed to be forced. I will breathe after my own fashion. Let us see who is the strongest.

- Henry David Thoreau, American Author

We manage
To remain mysteries
And strangers
To ourselves.
Traveling
As tourists
In our own internal terrains.
Often only pondering
And pursuing
From the perimeter –
Psuedo, surface, superficial –
Always partial
And foreign
To our own freedom.

What the superior man seeks is in himself; what the small man seeks is in others.

- Confucius

As Osho states, "Intimacy means exposing yourself before a stranger – and we are all strangers; nobody knows anybody. We are even strangers to ourselves because we don't know who we are. We are all hiding a thousand and one things, not only from others but from ourselves." Intimacy begins by removing the million masks we wear to hide our hate, habits, hurt and hardships; to cover-up the lies that we lean and count on to superficially secure our self-esteem.

I found out that there weren't too many limitations, if I did it my way.

Intimacy
Is internal intercourse
With the Invisible,
The Infinite
And the Immeasurable –
Without interference
Of mind,
Ego
Or external enticements.

Today you are You, that is truer than true. There is no one alive who is Youer than You.

- *Dr. Seuss, Happy Birthday to You!*

Inch by inch,
We gain insight
Into the intent
Of our internal instruments –
Intuition, instincts, intelligence –
And we start to innovate
From that database
Of depth.

Creativity is intelligence having fun.

- *Albert Einstein*

Intimacy strengthens when we are no longer concerned with fabricating an isolated identity, personality or image. All separation ceases, we are no longer divided. When these layers of ego and fabrications are removed, we become integrated and intense, and then all manipulation is muted. We are in an informational age; we are intellectually infatuated with information. We are overwhelmed and often overindulge in information but information is external and is inherently inaccurate and inflammatory in society. We cannot be internally instructed by information, intellect alone cannot penetrate our inner map; intuition is needed. Intuition is our inner guide, the instrument that initiates intelligence. "Intelligence," as Osho describes, "Is simply the ability to respond." Intelligence is responding to the present moment by going inwards, not reacting from old beliefs, scriptures or

207

accumulated knowledge from the past. Intelligence is fresh, new, alive and spontaneous; it does not come from texts, templates or terminology. Focus on the "in" not the "I" in intimacy, intensity, intelligence, integration and individuality.

The only way out is IN.

To be intimate,
One must go in.
We must make an incision.
Cut deep
Into the symphony
Of our silence
And be seduced
By that song
That only sings to us.

But if you do go in,
It will undoubtedly
Be uncomfortable,
Untamed
And unfamiliar.
It can and will
Get messy.

Being the richest man in the cemetery doesn't matter to me. Going to bed at night saying we've done something wonderful...that's what matters to me.

- Steve Jobs, Founder of Apple Computers

Therefore,
We must invest
In our I.R.A.

I.R.A = Internalization. Relation. Adaptation.

Internalize the music, movements and miracles of each moment as it unfolds. Feel and flourish with your own intensity and intelligence; forget what everyone else is doing, thinking or saying. Involve yourself, not through ignorance but through an illuminated innocence, an emptiness that embodies essence, not explanations. We are not robots or computers. Machines are efficient and can process inventory and information but they cannot internalize, interact or create on its own. Society molds us to be productive and efficient, mirroring machines, merely mechanical, reacting from the surface but never creating or responding from our inner guide, from intelligence. We remain cold like machines, isolated, never integrated. Internalize and be informed internally, not just outwardly.

When there is freedom from mechanical conditioning, there is simplicity. The classical man is just a bundle of routine, ideas and tradition. If you follow the classical pattern, you are understanding the routine, the tradition, the shadow — you are not understanding yourself.

- Bruce Lee

We must always be in the process of relating. Relating is a moment-to-moment response. Receiving information is not transformation. We must fully feel, taste, smell, experience and relate to each moment. We have the privilege to be totally, completely and wholeheartedly engaged in the extraordinary eloquence of everyday expressions, emotions and energy. How you were relating to a painting or a problem yesterday may not be the same way you relate to it today. Do not offer robotic or conditioned responses to what is alive, to what is new. Racism is a conditioned response, it is mechanical; it is rooted in the past and in ignorance and does not allow a person to experience something new. Racism is a surface reaction, whereas, relating is penetrating into the poetry of a person, place or process.

Understanding oneself happens through a process of relationships and not through isolation. To know oneself is to study oneself in action with another person.

- Bruce Lee

Relating leads to adapting. Adapting is the art of artistically accepting and responding to what is available, accessible and applicable in the present moment. We accept what *is* and then we improvise. Everything is constantly changing; it is when we stay stuck, stale and the same that we suffer and soak in sadness, starvation and suicide. Adapting is the answer.

It's not the strongest of the species that survive, nor the most intelligent, but the one most responsive to change.

- Charles Darwin

Intimacy
Begins with an invitation.
Invite the Invisible,
The Infinite,
And the Immeasurable.
Open the door,
Notice what we notice
And even notice
What we don't notice.
Involve
The involuntary –
Heartbeat, digestion, growth –
And integrate all that is invaluable
To your individuality.

Drop the idea of becoming someone, because you already are a masterpiece. You cannot be improved, you only have to come to it, to know it, to realize it.

- Osho

Bachata Bond: We often associate intimacy with distance. The closer we are, the more intimate we become with something. But intimacy is not so much about distance and proximity as it is integration. To be internally integrated is to be intimate, intense and illuminated.

Intimacy is a vital underlying element of Bachata. By simply being close with someone does not serve as any indication that intimacy has been established. Many male dancers misconstrue that dancing close means being intimate, but often times, no matter how close two bodies are, you will see someone completely disengaged, not interested or uncomfortable.

The highest levels of intimacy for a Bachatero, is to detach from all insecurities and self-consciousness, to fully and wholeheartedly, attend to your partner's artistry, caress her curiosities and to dissolve and disappear into her dance so that your dialogue, energy and essence echoes into eternity.

210

Bow. Breathe. Baila Bachata.

RELAXING. Relaxing is the art of enjoying a romance with our natural rhythms in relation to the present moment. Relax, and you will realize that all rules, reasons and roadblocks that have restricted our realities were all just invitations for reinvention.

Your power is proportional to your ability to relax.

- David Allen, American Author

The typical trademarks
Of a tough guy –
Territorial,
Tense
And troubled;
Often too rigid,
Rough
And robotic to relax.

The stiffest tree is the first to crack in the storm.

- Lao Tzu

We have been reduced to rat-racing robots. We are ruthlessly and restlessly running around to remain relevant in the roles, ranks and reputations that we reluctantly rely on. As the old saying goes, "If you win the rat race, you're still a rat." We are absolutely repressed by mundane repetition and disgusted with what we do on a daily basis, with whom we do it with and where we do it. So why do we continue doing what we are doing? Why are we surprised that sickness, sadness and suicide still saturate our societies, souls and spirits? We are burdened, anxious, easily embarrassed and have completely contaminated the natural narratives of our nervous system. We have unconsciously condemned and crippled the creativity, connectivity and consciousness of our bodies, breath, bones and blood.

Mourning every morning
Over our mindless missions
To make money –
Uptight,
Tense
And terrified
By all that is untamed;

We remain unresponsive
To nature's rewards
And riches.

Overreaching,
Rude
And sadly recycling the roots
Of recession,
We are often merely reduced to rent,
Rumors
Resumes and our ridiculous
Renderings of reality.
We repeatedly ridicule,
Renounce
And wrestle with our right
To receive.

Tension is who you think you should be, relaxation is who you are.

- Chinese Proverb

We are always tense, tight, tired and tangled up in tenacity of our temptations and the possessiveness of our temporary treasures. We are tormented by the tendencies of our tongue, talking tirelessly to translate our toughness, our sense of worth, our entitlement to what we eagerly and egotistically envision. This constant proving, chasing, climbing and relentless reaching to reinforce our relevance, is the root cause of the burdens we bear and bring to our bodies. The remedy is relaxing. *Tranquilo* and trust, through the ancient Indian art and tradition of Tantra.

The first thing is to learn respect for your body, to unlearn all the nonsense that has been taught to you about your body. Otherwise you will never turn on, and you will never turn in, and you will never turn beyond. Tantra teaches you to reclaim respect for the body, love for the body.

- Osho

Relaxing, as Tantra explains, is not merely a physical phenomenon of loosening up, not caring or simply resting your limbs. Tantra is the ultimate quality of relaxation as it is, first and foremost, an intimate invitation to trust your body, to enter it, to celebrate it. It is a total release of all restrictions, burdens and blockages in the body; an elimination of the ego. Tantra is pure naturalness. It is a complete and total awareness and acceptance of yourself as you are. There is no attitude, aspirations, anxiety or answers to assign to this acceptance and there is nothing to go against it. There is nothing to control, criticize, condemn or fight; only to free, feel and flourish.

Tantra begins with the basics – the beauty and breath of the body, that is why sex and sexuality are often the centralized focus and theme. Tantra is not a philosophy, or doctrine or of anything intellectual. Tantra literally means "method" or "technique" and serves as a map to experience your path to truth, to oneness, to total and utter relaxation. Tension affects both our intention and attention; therefore, both are constantly compromised and confined to the conditionings of society. The ailments, afflictions, diseases and disorders that we are diagnosed with are endless. The constant stress and struggles of society have adversely altered our natural state of relaxation. At a basic level, relaxation can be explored with the example of when a word or an idea is at the tip of your tongue. No matter how hard you concentrate or try to remember, you will not be able to say or express what you had intended. Then, moments later, when you are relaxed and not thinking about it, it comes to you. This is a glimpse into the Gift, the Gift of Godliness. A glimpse to remind you that you are in the way, remove yourself and relax into the rhythms of right now, allow the unknown to unravel. Receive these rhythms by relating, respecting and relaxing into them, not by rejecting or interfering with them.

Boxing great and legend, Floyd Mayweather, Jr., rests his entire repertoire of skills and strategy on the roots of relaxation. Where other brutes and brawlers are rough, wild, rigid and robotic, Floyd is refined, rhythmic and ready to retreat, attack or advance. He is fully alert, aware, accepting and attentive to every possibility in every situation, never stiff, never stuck. Boxing like life is spontaneous, anything can happen at any moment. He does not resist what *is* and never relies on what should or might be; remaining relaxed in the present moment, he is fully engaged and his energy is effortless. Before every fight, he always says, "It's going to be, what it's going to be." He has attentively and artistically accepted himself, the task at hand and the mysteries and magic of the moment. He is ready to respond.

Poised for prosperity
But perpetually positioned
For panic,
Paranoia
And pain.

Always rehearsing
But never responding.
We must not be tense
In a transient world.
Tranquility
And trust
Within our temples
Can only triumph
Through the awareness
That we have arrived;
Not through anxiety,
Anguish
Or aimless aggression.

Paintings by master artist, Vincent van Gogh, were originally deemed elementary to many, especially so-called experts, because his trees would reach the skies, everything was touching everything, lights from houses were touching the rivers, stars were swirls that touched mountains; nothing made sense and few, if any, were able to comprehend his work. Even though van Gogh never sold one painting during his lifetime, he remained undeterred to paint his visions and dreams. He was deeply rooted in his own reality. Now we all realize that he was right – energy and essence are both all-encompassing, pulsating and permeates all. Everything is connected.

Relax into your being, whoever you are. Don't impose any ideals. Don't drive yourself crazy; there is no need. Be – drop becoming.

- Osho

When one is relaxed,
There is nowhere to run.
No more racing,
Roaming

215

Or resisting.
Mind and movement
Are no longer impeded
By the motives of the masses.
Beyond a forced
Or contrived quality of cool
And calm,
Relaxation is a special space
Of supreme sincerity,
Stillness
And silence.
Responding by relaxing
Is to respect the Way.

Like van Gogh,
We can reroute the roadmaps
And routines of all that is true,
Tried and tested
And reinvent a romance
With the rhythms of our own realities.

Zen Masters are known to deliberately bring their students to points of maximum internal doubt, despair, tension and anxiety, knowing that a full surrendering will soon follow; a state of complete and utter acceptance and relaxation. Through physical, psychological, and spiritual exhaustion, by means of entering and enduring the extremes of emotional engagement and duress, a student is certain to dissolve into silence, stillness and spontaneity; releasing all restrictions and becoming receptive to the nature of things – working with the Way. Guitar strings must have tension to free its music, but it must be struck with complete and total relaxation. This is the understanding of Yin and Yang, the notion that there is tension in relaxation and relaxation in tension. Most people usually stiffen up, become terrified, desperate, compulsive or forceful at the first signs of fear, adversity, anger or anxiety. This is usually when things get even worse. We seek immediate relief, through mantras, methods and massage, but those solutions serve merely as an escape, a form of hypnosis. To fully and authentically relax and respond is to take responsibility and respect the reservoirs of our deepest dimensions of being. A fruit will naturally fall from a tree when it is ripe. Until then, the fruit is hard, bitter, raw and clinging to the tree. There is never any rush or resistance from the fruit; it simply relaxes.

Don't seek, don't search, don't ask, don't knock, don't demand –
relax. If you relax, it comes. If you relax, it is there. If you relax,
you start vibrating with it.

- Osho

Bachata Bond: Take a moment to observe and watch everyday, ordinary people doing everyday, ordinary things on the train, in cafes, malls, offices and on the streets. Chances are that you will notice blank eyes, heads down and bodies rushing and roaming aimlessly – anxious, nervous, tired, tense, irritated and desperate. We attempt to be "calm," composed and collected, but our inner narrative reveals differently.

How can we relax with so much uncertainty plaguing our daily lives? We are uncertain about everything – finances, futures, food, relationships, jobs – and nothing ever changes. The more we rush and resist, the more we remain unresponsive to our lives and to the Universe. This pertains to dancing Bachata as well. We cannot be fully responsive to our partners if we are not completely relaxed. Your signals will not be clear if you are tense, timid or tight and you will not feel anything that she is doing either. In dance, as in life, you must first relax and remove all the restrictions, limitations, worries and habits that adversely alter your responsiveness.

Bow. Breathe. Baila Bachata

RECOVERING AND HEALING. The road to recovering and healing is rooted in a full return to nature and our original essence.

We must turn to nature itself, to the observations of the body in health and in disease to learn the truth.

- Hippocrates, Greek Philosopher

Bargaining with our bodies,
Blindly bypassing
And bulldozing
Our way through barriers
And blockages,
Thus,
Our bodies
Become burdens.

Pain is inevitable, suffering is optional.

- Haruki Murakami, Japanese Author

Once the body becomes a burden,
We become beggars.
Begging for benefits,
For better this
And brighter that
While continuing to bruise,
Batter
And belittle our bodies –
Remaining broken
By our neurosis to be known,
Our desperation to be defined
And our anxiety
To be artificially accepted,
Applauded
And admired.

We have become more impersonal, impolite, impatient and imbalanced than ever. We often find ourselves unprepared, uncomfortable and unsettled in a cyclical, transient and ever-changing world. We are off-balanced because we have hardened into hurtful habits – repeating and repackaging predicaments from the past; recycling and succumbing to the same circumstances that leaves you stranded in sadness, sickness, starvation and suicide. We have been uprooted from the soil that makes our spirit sing. A tree that has been uprooted can no longer grow. It can take up space and merely exist but death and decay are now imminent. We must recover by relaxing and reclaiming our responsibilities to constantly refine, renew and rejuvenate our natural rhythms. We do so, not through resistance or resentment but by returning to the basics – to balance.

I visited many places, some of them quite exotic and far away, but I always returned to myself.

- Dejan Stojanovic, Serbian Poet

The brilliance of balance
Rests not
In our little ratios
And obsessions
To fabricate formulas;
Flurrying
To fit in family,
Fortune
And fitness.

Breathing out contacts the root of heaven, breathing in contacts the root of the earth.

- Taoist Proverb

Breathing –
Our bond with our breath
Is the breakthrough
To balance.

When you don't hear it, the breathing is fine; and when breathing is fine, the mind is clear. If you can hear it, the breathing is rough, which means the mind is cloudy.

- The Secret of the Golden Flower

Our breath is the blade
That slashes
Through all the physical,
Psychological
And spiritual symptoms
That plagues

219

And stiffens
Our natural states
Of free flowing vitality.

The brevity of our breath –
Short
And shallow;
Constantly shortchanging
The potency
And potential of our presence.

Fall down seven times. Stand up eight.

- Chinese Proverb

Breathing, like Bachata, is a whole body phenomenon. Lao Tzu describes the developed and enlightened man as one who "breathes from his heels" symbolizing the depth and totality of one's being. Most of us breathe from the chest or even the throat, so our breathing is limited and isolated to interactions between just nose and mouth. We are always short of breath, therefore, we are constantly falling short in life. Notice the poetry of pace by bringing your attention to your breathing when you are happy, angry, ambitious, jealous or in love. We are commonly told that we only use ten percent of our brains, but we use even less than that of our breath. When our breathing is full, expansive and mindfully circulated throughout our entire bodies, we no longer have to strive to find balance – we *are* balance. By *being* balance, we return to oneness, the original essence – our center.

Our culture made a virtue of living only as extroverts. We discouraged the inner journey, the quest for a center. So we lost our center and have to find it again.

- Anais Nin

Returning
And rekindling
The sincerity
And serenity of our center
Is to restore
The natural Way.

Return means seeing the heart of heaven and earth.

       - I-Ching, The Book of Changes

Our breath
Is the underlying source
That unifies
Our soul and spirit
Also serving
As the bridge
To the breath and pulse
Of our Universe.
Taoist Masters
Call this the "true breath."

You have now stabilized
In the center;
No longer scattered,
Split
Or struggling.

to the Universe –
It is the bridge
To the breath
And pulse of our Universe.

        Life begins within the mother,
    as the Universe is the mother of all things.
        Understanding the mother
    Makes it easier to understand the children,
         Watching the children
       we can know the mother better.

               - Lao Tzu

As we return
And unite
The Universe;
Our Mother,
Miracle-maker –
Mysterious and magical,
We are reborn
Into the natural roots
And rhythms
Of our original essence.

We have returned home.

The painter has the Universe in his mind and hands.

- Leonardo da Vinci, Artist

Bachata Bond: You would be surprised at how many people hold their breath when they dance. Holding your breath or taking shallow breaths while dancing is just as unhealthy, unbalanced and restrictive as it is in life. Free your breathing and bridge it to the breath and pulse of your partner, the music and the moment. Allow the dance of Bachata to gently lead you back to yourself.

Bow. Breathe. Baila Bachata.

CHILDREN. The peace, potential and poetry within each child rests solely in our promise to protect its purity.

Each second we live is a new and unique moment of the universe, a moment that will never be again. And what do we teach our children? We teach them that two and two make four, and that Paris is the capital of France. When will we also teach them what they are? We should say to each of them: Do you know what you are? You are a marvel. You are unique. In all the years that have passed, there has never been another child like you. Your legs, your arms, your clever fingers, the way you move. You may become a Shakespeare, a Michelangelo, a Beethoven. You have the capacity for anything. Yes, you are a marvel.

- Pablo Picasso

How will we guide our children? Gently and generously or through guilt and greed? Will we plot to define them by imposing our ignorant ideals or will we give them the tools to travel and define themselves? Will we abandon their artistic aspirations and spirit to selfishly steer them towards succumbing to the superficial standards of society? Will we take responsibility to protect their peace, purity and potential or will we merely position them to perpetuate poverty?

Every child comes with the message that God is not yet discouraged of man.

- Rabindranath Tagore, Bengali Poet

Forget not
That we are all children
To someone,
And our influence,
Attention
And awareness
To the challenges
And choices
Of our children today
Are literally
The triumphs
Of our tomorrow.

Look into the eyes of a child, you cannot find anything deeper.
The eyes of a child are an abyss, there is no bottom to them.

- Osho

Bachata Bond: Bachateros have a responsibility to share the dance of Bachata with our children. Children are natural Zen masters. They are uninhibited and in the moment – spontaneous, creative, curious and courageous. Bachata must be profoundly transmitted to them in this very manner; without bias, boredom or baggage.

Bow. Breathe. Baila Bachata.

ALL DAY. EVERYDAY. Bachata everyday, keeps both the devil and the doctor away.

Your dojo is everywhere.

- Zen Proverb

From Saturday celebrations
To sexy studios,
From bars
To the beach,
Your home
To your heart –
Bachata ,
Like the Tao,
Permeates the poetry
Of all forms of life.

Bachata,
Is not just a metaphor
Or movement
To music.
It is, ultimately,
The art of living.

The beat
Is embedded to the body,
Blood
And bones.
The evolving expressions
Of energy,
Culture
And emotion
Are a testament
To devotion.
Everyday is a dance,
Not just to music
But in every moment.

You must understand the whole of life, not just one little part of it. That is why you must read, that is why you must look at the skies, that is why you must sing and dance, and write poems, and suffer, and understand, for all that is life.

- J. Krishnamurti

A *karateka* (kah-rah-tekka) is a practitioner of the traditional Japanese martial art of Karate. In Japanese, the word *Karate* is broken up into *kara* (empty) and *te* (hand), or originally referred to as the art of the empty fist or bare hand. Similarly, a *judoka* (ju-doh-kah) is a practitioner of Judo, another traditional form of Japanese martial arts, meaning "the gentle way," where one does not resist but rather relaxes and reduces the force or power of an opponent's attack by allowing, following and flowing with it, thus, achieving maximum efficiency, with minimum effort. For both the karateka and the judoka, their martial mastery was meant to extend into the responsibilities, expressions and excellence of everyday engagements. As Gichin Funakoshi, the Founder of Shotokan Karate said, "The ultimate aim of karate lies not in victory nor defeat, but in the perfection of the character of its participants." With this same spirit and sincerity, the Bachatero follows the Way of Bachata to enrich our environment – psychologically, socially, artistically, spiritually and sensually.

Bow. Breathe. Baila Bachata.

FINISHING. Many will hope, wish, pray and work – but few will ever witness their fight take flight. We fail to fly because we fail to finish.

Anybody can make you enjoy the first bite of a dish, but only a real chef can make you enjoy the last.

- *Francois Minot, French Chef*

We are a culture
Of unclaimed creativity.
Rarely do we redeem
Our natural rights
To riches
And rewards,
Leaving romances
And relationships
Unrealized;
Dying
With dialogues,
Dreams
And determination
Still screaming
To be shared.

We frequently fail
En route to what we envision.
Flat lined
Before the finish line;
Leaving stories untold,
Stones unturned
And strengths untested.

People often fail on the verge of success.
By giving as much care to the end as to the beginning,
There will be few failures.

- Tao Te Ching

The end result is what intrigues us. We love the shiny look of "making it" – seductive success and prosperity. We envision writing best-selling novels, opening celebrity-soaked restaurants, performing in sold-out stadiums and implementing the next big idea to technologically advance the world. But we often fall short, fall apart and falter in the fields of our fantasies. Why?

The *enso* circle is a sacred symbol of Zen Buddhism. The enso circle is an open-ended circle that is usually expressed by one continuous brush stroke. The enso is a widely used in schools, scriptures, books, design and everyday life to symbolize the beginning and end of all things. The enso embodies emptiness and fullness, presence and absence and the harmonious oneness of all Existence. Few masters, teachers, painters or artists have been able to fulfill the spirit, sincerity or spontaneity of drawing an enso circle. With one simple brushstroke, all is revealed and exposed – purity of heart, skill and mastery of the moment. In order to fully engage, express and experience the beginnings and endings of our existence – relationships, businesses, art – we must draw inspiration from the openness and oneness of the enso circle. Be open to the imperfections and perfections of the moment, the light and dark, the existent and non-existent and rejoice in this oneness. We break down, weaken and quit when we close ourselves off and separate from the source of our oneness.

The beginning and end of the practice must be one.

- Lu-Tsu, Ancient Chinese Mystic

The End
Embodies a new beginning
And a new beginning
Embodies the end,
Your entry
Is your exit,
And your exit
Is your entry.
Evolve into this essence
In all your endeavors
And you will flourish
Way past far
And forever.

Therefore those skilled at the unorthodox are infinite as heaven and earth, inexhaustible as the great rivers. When they come to an end, they begin again. Like the days and months; they die and are reborn, like the four seasons.

Bachata Bond: Finish every dance, every move, every song and every moment. Go all-in. Dare to dance your dance and fly free with your flavor.

Bow. Breathe. Baila Bachata.

CONCLUSION

Our lives begin to end the day we become silent about things that matter.

- Dr. Martin Luther King, Jr.

Bachata matters.
More than a mere metaphor
Or abstract analogy,
Bachata gives access
To our own artistic
Abundance
And authority.

Mindless men
That have been molded
By the marketplace
Are merciless,
Manipulative
And malicious
But are now immaterial
And as impotent
As the impermanence
Of "impossible."

The era of elitist executives
And employers
Exercising their ego
And economic engines
To tame
And take the treasures
And triumphs of Man,
Has expired.

Capitalism
Is now conscious –
Capitalizing
On the courage,
Compassion
And creativity of Man,
Not the violence
And vulnerabilities
Of catastrophe and collapse.

The age of brutes
And barbarians are over;
Savages
Seeking to suffocate
The spirit,
Soul
And celebrations of Man
Have been sidelined
And stopped.

In a world that is constantly telling you that you are "not good enough," "not experienced enough" or "it's not your time yet," the art and dance of Bachata woke me up and allowed me to witness my own worth – to walk freely with the will, wisdom and wings that were woven deep within. I started opening to the purity, potential and promise of what was possible. I was no longer pushed or provoked to pursue the petty promotions, perversions or political prejudices of society. I did not desire to accumulate artificial accessories, accolades or approval and I adamantly refused to be reduced to any titles or roles. I was no longer an employee. I did not have to earn a living because I was now enjoying my living. I was not obligated to obey or obsess over my desk or the drama that came along with it. I did not entertain any egos, agendas or scandals; therefore, I was invincible and inaccessible to any forms of manipulation, exploitation or intimidation. Look around you and you will notice that most so-called executives, bosses and corporate cowards are obese, out of shape and outdated. They can maneuver the marketplace – managing, hiring, firing, making calls, controlling, posturing – but most are miserable, insecure, awkward and unhealthy. I no longer had to subject myself to their imbalances, dysfunctions and deficiencies.

Turn the tables
On the tyranny
And traps that society
Has employed to traumatize,
Torture
And tamper
With the fundamental faculties
Of our freedom.

Most of us are still asleep and on autopilot – completely accustomed to having people telling us what to do and when to do it during the course of our entire lives. The mechanical mentality of the masses – millions pushing, battling and killing to get through the same door; going through life violent, petty and desperate. But we do not have to marinate in this mess or be entangled in this energy. These are the conflicts, collisions and complexities of crowds and cowards. With consciousness, we are exempt from this commotion because we can now elevate into the enlightened levels of living, loving and creating through our own unique artistic angles and approaches to our everyday experiences.

A man really becomes a man when he accepts total responsibility – he is responsible for whatsoever he is. This is the first courage, the greatest courage.

- Osho

We have been wounded
But we are not worthless,
We do not need violence
To be victorious
And we do not need greed
To gain.

We must transform
And transcend
The currently malnourished
Manifesto of the modern man
By confronting
The contemporary conflicts,
Conditions
And contaminations
Of our culture
With a new hue of humanity.

No longer
Will the influences
And ideals of institutions,
Icons
And images
Overpower the profoundness
Of Individual inquiry,
Intimacy
And intensity.

The internal illumination
Of a man
Ignites integrity
And marks the beginning
Of a more meditative,
Mindful
And masterful man.

This is the birth
Of Buddha the Bachatero.

A blueprint
That exemplifies the enlightenment
Of a Buddha
And the emotions of a Bachatero –
Synthesizing stillness and silence
With sazon and sensuality,
Awareness with artistry,
Relaxation with romance
And freedom with fire.

As we banish all blame
And bickering,
We will start to bloom
With the presence of a Buddha
And the poetry of a Bachatero;
Dissolving
All the darkness
That has dictated the dismantling
Of our dreams,
Deeds
And dialogues
And finally realizing
That our existence
Was all a dance after all.

Is life serious?

No,
But it *is* sincere
And requires the sensitivity
Of a Buddha
And the celebrations of a Bachatero
To savor all of its subtleties.

The spirit and dance of Bachata is in our D.N.A. It is a universal language that translates and crosses all cultural, social and racial barriers. Bachata has contributed to musical, economical and artistic advancements and blesses us with a beat that permeates beyond the body and into our very breath, blood and bones. Bachata is a life-long devotion to the exploration, examination and evolution of our emotions, energy and expressions in relation to our wildest wishes, worries and women. We shall forever be seduced by the simplicity, spontaneity and sensuality of Bachata.

The minute I stopped trying to find the right girl, and started trying to become the right guy...the girl came.

- Jonathan Antin, Author

As the modern man begins to embody the essence of Buddha the Bachatero – from Manhattan to Medellin, Brooklyn to Brazil, L.E.S. to L.A., the Dominican Republic to Rome and from Washington Heights to worldwide – a revival and reinvention of our roles and responsibilities will rise towards the wellness of our women. We will devote ourselves to the dreams and dimples of our daughters, celebrate the sincerity and soul of our sisters, gather gratitude for the grace and greatness of our grandmothers and continue to walk the Way with our women warriors. As I continue to look into the eyes of our women all across the globe and embrace their energies, emotions and expressions through the dance of Bachata, I have attained the awareness that whether you believe in god, animals or chocolate, there is hope for a harmonious and heartfelt humanity. But much work is needed. This is the work of Buddha the Bachatero.

I don't know what that dream is that you have, I don't care how disappointing it might have been as you have been working toward that dream, but here's what I know, that that dream that you're holding in your mind, that it's possible.

- Les Brown, Motivational Speaker

Bow. Breathe. Baila Bachata.

About the Author

Franko is a contemporary collector of creative consciousness, energy and emotions. He shares this collection through his vision and reinvention of the modern man, branded "Buddha the Bachatero." Buddha the Bachatero is the embodiment of the Eastern engine illuminated by Latin limbs, lyrics and love. By combining the silence and stillness of a Buddha and the sensuality and sazon of a Bachatero – synthesizing awareness and artistry, presence and poetry, eternal energy and emotions – we can profoundly penetrate the most pressing social, economical and artistic challenges that we face today in our relationships, businesses and daily lives. Franko continues to write, dance and travel all across the globe to heal and harmonize the hearts, hands, homes and humor of humanity through the musical genre and dance of Bachata along with the timeless treasures and teachings of Eastern wisdom and philosophy.

For more information please visit
www.buddhathebachatero.com